PRESIDENT NEXT

A HISTORICAL ROADMAP TO FORECASTING THE FUTURE PRESIDENT

DAVID CARLUCCI

First Paperback and Hardback Edition

Published by Freiling Agency, LLC.

P.O. Box 1264
Warrenton, VA 20188

www.FreilingAgency.com

HB ISBN: 978-1-969826-06-1
PB ISBN: 978-1-969826-05-4
E-book ISBN: 978-1-969826-07-8

CONTENTS

Introduction....v

1 Kennedy Surge (1960)....1

2 McCarthy Shock (1968)....11

3 McGovern Insurgency (1972)....21

4 Carter Miracle (1976)....33

5 Kennedy Challenge (1980)....45

6 Hart Attack (1984)....57

7 Jackson Rainbow (1988)....69

8 Comeback Kid (1992)....81

9 Buchanan Brigades (1996)....93

10 McCain Surge (2000)....105

11 Dean Scream (2004)....119

12 Obama Phenomenon (2008)....133

13 Santorum Surge (2012)....145

14 Trump Tidal Wave (2016)....159

15 Buttigieg Boomlet (2020)....173

16 Haley Flash (2024)....187

Conclusion....199

“Understanding presidential primaries requires appreciating this fundamental tension between breakthrough and sustainability.”

INTRODUCTION

On a frigid February night in 1968, Eugene McCarthy's volunteers huddled around television sets in New Hampshire hotel rooms, watching returns trickle in from polling stations across the Granite State. Pundits had dismissed the Minnesota senator as a quixotic anti-war candidate with no chance against an incumbent president. Yet as the numbers climbed—20 percent, then 35, then an astonishing 42 percent against Lyndon Johnson's 49—something unprecedented was happening. Within hours, the political universe had shifted on its axis. Four weeks later, Johnson announced he would not seek reelection.

McCarthy's near-victory that night represents one of the most dramatic examples of what this book calls a "breakthrough moment"—those pivotal instances when an underdog candidate suddenly captures the nation's attention, reshapes the political conversation, and threatens to upend the entire presidential race. These breakthroughs are the shooting stars of American politics: brilliant, unexpected, and capable of illuminating the entire political sky, if only briefly.

But here lies the central paradox of presidential primaries: the candidates who create the most excitement, generate the most headlines, and spark the most passionate followings are rarely the ones who ultimately secure their party's nomination. For every Barack Obama who transforms a breakthrough into sustained success, there are dozens of Gary Harts, Howard Deans, and Rick Santorums who blaze across the political firmament only to burn out before reaching their destination.

The modern presidential primary system, born from the ashes of the chaotic 1968 Democratic Convention, was designed to democratize the nomination process and give voters a direct voice in selecting their party's standard-bearer. What the reformers didn't anticipate was how this new system would create a unique ecosystem where breakthrough moments could flourish—and where the very qualities that enable a candidate to break through might also prevent them from building the broad, durable coalition necessary to win.

The story of presidential primaries over the past six decades is, fundamentally, the story of this tension between breakthrough and sustainability. It's the difference between catching lightning in a bottle and harnessing that energy for the long haul. It's the distinction between being a movement and leading a party.

Consider the pattern: In 1972, George McGovern harnessed anti-war fervor and new party rules to leap from 2 percent in early polls to the Democratic nomination, only to suffer one of the worst general election defeats in American history. In 1984, Gary Hart's "new ideas" campaign stunned Walter Mondale in New Hampshire and briefly made him the Democratic frontrunner, until questions about substance and organization derailed his insurgency. In 2004, Howard Dean revolutionized political fundraising and grassroots organizing through the internet, generating unprecedented enthusiasm among young voters, only to see his campaign collapse after a single poor showing in Iowa.

Each of these candidates mastered the art of the breakthrough but failed to solve the puzzle of sustainability. They could ignite, but they couldn't endure.

What creates these breakthrough moments? After analyzing sixteen of the most significant primary insurgencies since 1960, several patterns emerge. First, breakthrough candidates almost always emerge from outside the traditional power structure of their party. They're senators rather than governors, outsiders rather than establishment figures, representatives of new constituencies rather than traditional coalitions.

Second, they possess what political scientists call "asymmetric advantages"—unique strengths that allow them to compete despite resource disadvantages. John McCain had his "Straight Talk Express" and media relationships. Barack Obama had superior organization and inspirational rhetoric. Donald Trump had celebrity status and an intuitive understanding of television. These advantages allow breakthrough candidates to punch above their weight class, at least initially.

Third, breakthrough moments require what military strategists call "operational surprise"—the ability to exceed expectations dramatically in a highly visible contest. The New Hampshire primary has traditionally served this function, rewarding candidates who can mobilize independent voters and generate disproportionate media attention. Iowa's caucuses, with their emphasis on organization and intensity, have played a similar role.

Finally, breakthrough candidates typically embody or articulate a message that resonates with their party's zeitgeist. They don't just run against their opponents; they run against the conventional wisdom, the establishment, or the status quo. They represent change, even when they can't always define what that change might look like.

Yet breakthrough and sustainability require different skill sets, different resources, and often different messages. The insurgent energy that fuels a breakthrough can become a liability when trying to build a broad coalition. The anti-establishment message that works in New Hampshire may fall flat in South Carolina. The small-dollar fundraising that powers early success may prove insufficient for Super Tuesday's expensive, multi-state battles.

Moreover, breakthrough candidates face what this book terms "the establishment counterattack"—the inevitable response from party leaders, major donors, and institutional players who mobilize to prevent the insurgent from capturing the nomination. This counterattack can take many forms: endorsements consolidating around a preferred alternative, negative advertising highlighting the insurgent's vulnerabilities, or simply the weight of institutional support tilting toward more traditional candidates.

The candidates who successfully navigate from breakthrough to nomination—figures like Jimmy Carter, Bill Clinton, Barack Obama, and Donald Trump—share certain characteristics. They combine insurgent energy with pragmatic coalition-building. They maintain their breakthrough message while expanding their appeal. Most importantly, they build organizations capable of sustaining success across multiple contests and over many months.

The nature of breakthrough moments has evolved dramatically as the media landscape has transformed. In 1960, John Kennedy's breakthrough required proving himself in just two primaries, Wisconsin and West Virginia, before an elite press corps that could anoint or destroy candidacies with a few well-placed stories. By 2020, Pete Buttigieg's breakthrough required navigating a fragmented media ecosystem where cable news, social media, and traditional outlets all played different roles in shaping public perception.

The rise of cable television created new opportunities for breakthrough candidates to build national profiles, but it also accelerated the news cycle and shortened attention spans. Social media has democratized political communication, but it has also made it harder to control the narrative and message. The internet has revolutionized fundraising and organizing, but has also made vetting and opposition research more brutal and immediate.

Each technological shift has created new paths to breakthrough while closing off others. Howard Dean's internet-powered insurgency seemed revolutionary in 2004 but was quickly adopted by all subsequent campaigns. Donald Trump's Twitter-driven media strategy dominated 2016 but may prove less effective as platforms change and audiences fragment.

Why does this pattern matter? Because understanding the dynamics of breakthrough and sustainability offers crucial insights into American democracy itself. Presidential primaries are where parties define themselves, where new leaders emerge, and where the political system demonstrates its capacity for renewal and change. They're also where voters get their first sustained look at potential presidents, making judgments about character, competence, and vision that will shape the general election and, potentially, the next four years of American governance.

The candidates who break through in primaries often represent important constituencies or ideas that might otherwise be marginalized. Eugene McCarthy gave voice to anti-war sentiment. Jesse Jackson articulated the aspirations of minority voters. Pat Buchanan channeled economic populism. Howard Dean energized young progressives. These breakthrough moments, even when they don't lead to nominations, often influence party platforms, shape policy debates, and elevate issues that might otherwise be ignored.

At the same time, the failure of breakthrough candidates to sustain their success raises important questions about the primary system itself. Does the current structure reward the right qualities in potential presidents? Do the skills required to break through align with those needed to govern effectively? Are we selecting for electoral performance or governing competence?

This book examines sixteen breakthrough moments across both parties from 1960 to 2024, analyzing what enabled each candidate to capture lightning in a bottle and why some were able to hold onto it while others saw it slip away. Each chapter tells the story of a specific breakthrough—the candidate, the moment, the context, and the consequences—while building toward a broader understanding of how American presidential politics really works.

We'll explore how John Kennedy used two strategic primary victories to overcome religious prejudice and establish himself as a serious contender. We'll see how Jimmy Carter parlayed obscurity into an asset, turning his outsider status into a powerful message about change and renewal. We'll watch Barack Obama transform a single Iowa victory into a movement that redefined American politics. And we'll examine how Donald Trump shattered traditional assumptions about what it takes to win a presidential nomination.

We'll also analyze the shooting stars who burned bright but brief: Gary Hart's "new ideas" insurgency, Howard Dean's internet revolution, Pete Buttigieg's generational appeal. What can these near-misses teach us about the difference between breaking through and breaking out?

The central argument of this book is that understanding presidential primaries requires appreciating this fundamental tension between breakthrough and sustainability. The system rewards disruption but demands consolidation. It celebrates insurgents but nominates coalition-builders. It values authenticity but requires adaptability.

For political junkies seeking to understand how American presidential politics really works, for campaign professionals trying to navigate the path to power, and for citizens wondering how we choose our leaders, this tension between shooting stars and sustained success offers the key to unlocking the mysteries of the primary process.

The story begins in 1960, when a young senator from Massachusetts decided to prove that Catholics could win in Protestant America. His breakthrough would establish the template for modern presidential campaigns and demonstrate that in American politics, sometimes the most unlikely candidates can reach the highest office—if they can figure out how to turn a moment of brilliance into months of sustained success.

The shooting stars are about to take the stage.

“A breakthrough that would transform American politics, but it was only the beginning of Kennedy’s journey toward the nomination.”

1

KENNEDY SURGE (1960)

The snow was falling hard on the morning of April 5, 1960, as John F. Kennedy's motorcade wound through the working-class neighborhoods of Milwaukee. Inside his car, the 42-year-old senator from Massachusetts studied the latest polling data with growing concern. Despite months of campaigning in Wisconsin, he was locked in a virtual tie with Hubert Humphrey, the populist senator from neighboring Minnesota who seemed to embody everything Kennedy was not: older, more experienced, and blessed with the common touch that came naturally to a pharmacist's son from the heartland.

Kennedy's advisers had warned him against entering the Wisconsin primary. The Democratic establishment—led by party elders like Adlai Stevenson and Stuart Symington—preferred to settle the nomination through the traditional smoke-filled rooms of the national convention. Why risk everything on the uncertain terrain of primary elections, especially when Kennedy already faced whispered doubts about his youth, his religion, and his family's controversial wealth?

But Kennedy understood something that the establishment missed: the old system was dying. Television was transforming American politics, creating new opportunities for candidates who could master the medium. The primary process, long considered a sideshow to the real business of convention politics, was becoming the main event. Most importantly, Kennedy recognized that as a Catholic seeking the presidency—something no member of his faith had ever achieved—he needed to prove his electability in Protestant America. The primaries weren't just an option; they were his only path to the White House.

Kennedy's decision to compete in Wisconsin represented the first great strategic gamble of the modern primary era. Traditional wisdom suggested that a Catholic candidate should avoid testing his appeal in Protestant strongholds. Wisconsin, with its heavily Lutheran and German population, seemed particularly inhospitable territory. Humphrey, meanwhile, enjoyed every possible advantage: regional proximity, ideological affinity with Wisconsin's progressive tradition, and the support of organized labor.

Yet Kennedy's inner circle, led by his brother Bobby and political strategist Lawrence O'Brien, saw opportunity in this very disadvantage. If Kennedy could prove competitive in hostile territory, it would demonstrate a broad appeal that transcended traditional ethnic and religious boundaries. More importantly, it would establish him as the only candidate willing to submit his candidacy to the judgment of actual voters rather than party bosses.

The Kennedy campaign that took shape in Wisconsin bore little resemblance to the genteel operations that had characterized previous presidential contests. Drawing on lessons learned from JFK's successful 1958 Senate reelection campaign, the organization emphasized meticulous voter identification, sophisticated polling, and unprecedented family involvement. The candidate's photogenic wife, Jacqueline, his charismatic brothers Bobby and Ted, and even his parents joined the effort, creating a political dynasty in action that fascinated voters and media alike.

"We're not running a typical campaign," Bobby Kennedy told a gathering of Wisconsin volunteers in March 1960. "We're building a movement." It was an audacious claim for a candidate who had entered the race trailing badly in national polls. Still, it reflected the campaign's understanding that traditional metrics might not apply in this new primary-driven environment.

What truly distinguished Kennedy's Wisconsin operation was its sophisticated understanding of television's political potential. While other candidates still relied primarily on radio addresses and newspaper endorsements, Kennedy embraced the visual medium with the enthusiasm of a Hollywood producer. His campaign hired professional filmmakers to create polished television advertisements—a rarity in 1960—and scheduled events specifically designed for television coverage.

The contrast with Humphrey could not have been more stark. The Minnesota senator, operating on a shoestring budget, relied on his natural eloquence and policy expertise to connect with voters through traditional rallies and speeches. Kennedy, backed by his family's wealth and surrounded by Madison Avenue professionals, crafted a campaign that played to television's strengths: youth, vitality, and visual appeal.

This technological advantage became apparent during Kennedy's appearances on Wisconsin television stations. Where other politicians seemed stiff and uncomfortable in the television studio, Kennedy appeared natural and conversational. His handlers had learned to apply light makeup to reduce the glare from studio lights—a technique that would prove crucial in Kennedy's later debates with Richard Nixon—and coached him on the importance of speaking directly to the camera rather than to the interviewer.

Local television producers, hungry for content in an era when national programming dominated the airwaves, welcomed Kennedy's polished presentations. His campaign provided ready-made content that filled programming hours while serving its political objectives. It was a symbiotic relationship that would become the template for all subsequent presidential campaigns.

Behind the television glamour lay an organizational innovation that would reshape American political campaigning. The Kennedy operation in Wisconsin represented the first systematic application of modern market research techniques to presidential politics. Using data provided by pollster Lou Harris—himself a pioneer in political polling—the campaign identified persuadable voters with unprecedented precision.

Rather than relying on county chairmen and traditional party organizations, Kennedy's team built a parallel structure of volunteers recruited through personal networks, college campuses, and Catholic parishes. These volunteers were trained in specific techniques: how to identify Kennedy supporters through brief phone conversations, how to record voter preferences on standardized forms, and how to ensure that identified supporters actually voted on primary day.

The sophistication of this organizing effort impressed even seasoned political observers. Theodore White, whose "The Making of the President 1960" would establish the template for campaign journalism, noted that Kennedy's Wisconsin organization "operated with the precision of a Swiss watch and the enthusiasm of a revival meeting."

This organizational advantage became particularly apparent in Wisconsin's rural counties, where traditional campaigning relied heavily on relationships with local party leaders and union officials. Kennedy's volunteers, many of them young and idealistic, compensated for their lack of political experience with sheer energy and dedication. They knocked on doors in farming communities where presidential candidates rarely ventured, distributed literature in shopping centers and factory gates, and maintained telephone banks that operated from early morning until late evening.

Humphrey, despite his regional advantages, struggled to match this organizational intensity. His campaign relied heavily on labor union support and traditional Democratic party structures, but these proved insufficient against Kennedy's volunteer army. As one Humphrey aide ruefully observed after the primary, "They out-organized us in our own backyard."

Underlying Kennedy's Wisconsin strategy was a calculation that would prove crucial throughout the 1960 campaign: rather than avoiding the religious question, he would confront it directly. Kennedy's advisers understood that his Catholicism would be an issue in any national campaign, so Wisconsin provided an opportunity to address Protestant concerns in a relatively low-stakes environment.

The strategy carried significant risks. Wisconsin's Protestant voters harbored deep suspicions about Catholic political loyalty, rooted in centuries of religious conflict and reinforced by more recent fears about Vatican influence in American politics. Anti-Catholic literature circulated throughout the state, warning that a Catholic president would take orders from the Pope and undermine the constitutional separation of church and state.

Kennedy's response was characteristically direct. Rather than soft-pedaling his religion or emphasizing his independence from church hierarchy, he spoke openly about his faith while making clear his commitment to constitutional principles. In a speech to the Milwaukee Press Club, he declared: "I am not the Catholic candidate for President. I am the Democratic Party's candidate for President who happens also to be a Catholic."

This approach served multiple purposes. It demonstrated Kennedy's willingness to address difficult questions directly—a quality that would serve him well in later debates with Nixon. It allowed him to position himself as a victim of religious prejudice, potentially generating sympathy votes from fair-minded Protestants. Most importantly, it began the process of normalizing the idea of a Catholic president, preparing the ground for later primary contests and the general election.

The religious dimension of the Wisconsin primary also revealed the complexity of Kennedy's appeal within his own faith community. While many Catholic voters supported him enthusiastically, others worried that his candidacy might provoke a backlash that would harm Catholic interests more broadly. Some Catholic leaders privately urged Kennedy to withdraw from the race rather than risk a defeat that might be interpreted as a rejection of Catholic political participation.

Kennedy rejected such counsel, understanding that retreat would effectively end any Catholic's presidential ambitions for a generation. "If we don't run now," he told a gathering of Catholic supporters, "when will we ever run?"

When Wisconsin voters went to the polls on April 5, 1960, Kennedy's gamble appeared to pay off. He defeated Humphrey by a margin of 56 percent to 44 percent, carrying six of the state's ten congressional districts. The victory made national headlines and established Kennedy as the Democratic frontrunner, demonstrating that a Catholic could win in Protestant territory.

Yet the victory proved more complicated than the headlines suggested. Kennedy's margin came primarily from heavily Catholic districts, while Humphrey carried most Protestant areas. Rather than resolving questions about Kennedy's electability, the Wisconsin results seemed to confirm fears that American politics was dividing along religious lines.

This geographic and religious polarization troubled Kennedy's advisers, who had hoped for a more convincing demonstration of broad appeal. The national media, meanwhile, interpreted the results through the lens of religious voting patterns, raising new questions about Kennedy's ability to unify the country. James Reston of the New York Times wrote that Kennedy's victory "raised as many questions as it answered about his chances in November."

More immediately, the Wisconsin results failed to drive Humphrey from the race, as Kennedy had hoped. Instead, the Minnesota senator vowed to continue his campaign, forcing Kennedy into another primary contest in West Virginia. This state was 95 percent Protestant and seemed even less hospitable to Catholic candidacy.

The Wisconsin primary had established Kennedy as a serious contender and demonstrated the potential of the new primary-focused campaign model. But it had not yet solved the fundamental challenge of his candidacy: proving that a Catholic could win Protestant votes in sufficient numbers to capture the presidency.

Regardless of its mixed political results, Kennedy's Wisconsin campaign established the template that would govern presidential primaries for decades to come. The emphasis on television, sophisticated polling, grassroots organizing, and direct voter contact became standard features of every subsequent campaign. The willingness to risk everything on primary elections rather than convention politics fundamentally altered the presidential selection process.

Kennedy's Wisconsin breakthrough also demonstrated the importance of managing expectations and controlling narrative in the media age. Despite winning decisively, Kennedy found himself defending the narrowness of his victory and the religious polarization it revealed. Future candidates would learn to set expectations carefully and prepare multiple interpretations of potential results.

Most significantly, the Wisconsin primary showed that breakthrough moments in the new system required sustained effort over many months rather than single dramatic events. Kennedy's victory was the product of organizational excellence, financial resources, and strategic vision rather than spontaneous voter enthusiasm. It was a different kind of breakthrough than the emotional insurgencies that would characterize later primary campaigns.

The Kennedy surge in Wisconsin represented the birth of the modern presidential campaign: professional, expensive, media-savvy, and dependent on primary victories rather than party endorsements. It was a breakthrough that would transform American politics, but it was only the beginning of Kennedy's journey toward the nomination.

The real test lay ahead in West Virginia, where a young Catholic senator would need to prove that his Wisconsin victory was more than just ethnic politics—that he could truly transcend the religious barriers that had constrained American presidential politics since the founding of the republic. In the coal fields and small towns of West Virginia, Kennedy would discover whether his breakthrough could evolve into something more: a sustainable path to the White House.

Lessons for Modern Candidates

Kennedy's Wisconsin breakthrough offers enduring insights for contemporary presidential candidates navigating today's primary landscape. While the media environment has evolved dramatically since 1960, the fundamental dynamics Kennedy mastered remain relevant.

First, Kennedy understood that technological disruption creates new pathways to breakthrough success. Just as he embraced television when other candidates clung to radio and newspapers, today's breakthrough candidates must identify and master emerging platforms before their competitors. Barack Obama's early adoption of social media organizing, Donald Trump's intuitive grasp of Twitter's political potential, and Pete Buttigieg's sophisticated use of digital fundraising all echo Kennedy's television strategy—finding asymmetric advantages through technological innovation.

Second, Kennedy demonstrated that perceived weaknesses can become sources of strength when addressed directly rather than avoided. His Catholicism, initially seen as disqualifying, became proof of his courage and authenticity when he confronted religious prejudice head-on. Modern candidates facing questions about age, experience, ideology, or background should note Kennedy's approach: embrace the challenge, define it on your own terms, and use it to demonstrate presidential qualities like honesty and resilience.

Third, the Wisconsin campaign revealed the critical importance of infrastructure over inspiration in primary politics. Kennedy's victory came not from soaring rhetoric or emotional rallies, but from superior organization, data-driven voter targeting, and systematic volunteer recruitment. Today's candidates who focus solely on generating excitement—without building the organizational capacity to identify, persuade, and turn out voters—risk following the path of Howard Dean rather than Barack Obama.

Fourth, Kennedy's experience illustrates the double-edged nature of primary victories in the media age. Success brings scrutiny, and breakthrough moments often reveal new vulnerabilities even as they demonstrate strength. Modern candidates must prepare not just to win, but to manage the aftermath of winning—controlling narratives, addressing weaknesses exposed by victory, and maintaining momentum despite increased opposition research and media attention.

Finally, Kennedy's Wisconsin campaign shows that breakthrough candidates must think beyond single contests to build sustainable coalitions. His religious polarization problem in Wisconsin foreshadowed challenges that would persist throughout his campaign and presidency. Today's candidates who achieve breakthrough success by appealing to narrow constituencies—whether ideological, generational, or demographic—must quickly demonstrate broader appeal or risk being marginalized as their initial breakthrough fades.

The Kennedy model remains the gold standard for transforming technological innovation, strategic risk-taking, and organizational excellence into political breakthroughs. But Wisconsin also warned of the challenges that lie ahead when breakthrough energy must be sustained across diverse constituencies and changing political terrain. Modern candidates ignore these lessons at their peril—the primary graveyard is littered with politicians who mastered the breakthrough but failed to solve the puzzle of sustainability that Kennedy would confront in the coal fields of West Virginia.

“McCarthy’s breakthrough established the template for insurgent campaigns that would follow: mobilize passionate activists.”

2

MCCARTHY SHOCK (1968)

The Secret Service agents seemed genuinely puzzled. It was January 1968, and they had been assigned to protect a presidential candidate who attracted crowds unlike anything they had experienced in conventional politics. Instead of the usual mix of party officials, local dignitaries, and curious onlookers, Eugene McCarthy's audiences consisted largely of college students who quoted poetry, debated foreign policy with sophisticated intensity, and approached politics with the fervor of a religious crusade.

"They don't look like regular Democrats," one agent confided to McCarthy's campaign manager, Blair Clark, after a particularly enthusiastic rally at the University of Wisconsin. Clark smiled grimly. That was precisely the point.

McCarthy's decision to challenge President Lyndon Johnson for the Democratic nomination represented the most audacious political gamble since the founding of the modern primary system. No senator had successfully challenged a sitting president of his own party since the advent of primaries. The political establishment considered such challenges not merely futile but treasonous—violations of party loyalty that threatened to weaken the eventual Democratic nominee against the Republicans.

Yet by March 12, 1968, when New Hampshire voters delivered their stunning verdict, McCarthy had accomplished something that political scientists had deemed impossible: he had transformed a protest candidacy into a legitimate threat to unseat a sitting president. His 42 percent showing against Johnson's 49 percent represented far more than a moral victory—it was a political earthquake that would reshape the Democratic Party and alter the course of American history.

Eugene McCarthy seemed an unlikely revolutionary. A former college professor and published poet, the Minnesota senator possessed an intellectual demeanor that often appeared detached from the rough-and-tumble of electoral politics. His colleagues in the Senate respected his intelligence and principles but questioned his political instincts. Even his supporters acknowledged that he lacked the emotional fire that typically drove successful presidential campaigns.

"Gene was not what you would call a natural politician," recalled Richard Goodwin, the former Kennedy speechwriter who joined McCarthy's campaign. "He was more interested in discussing the philosophical implications of American foreign policy than in working a rope line or remembering names at a fundraising dinner."

This cerebral approach initially made McCarthy's anti-war candidacy seem quixotic. The Vietnam War had indeed grown increasingly unpopular by 1967, but opposition remained concentrated among college students and liberal intellectuals—groups with limited political influence within the Democratic Party. Labor unions, ethnic organizations, and Southern Democrats continued to support Johnson's war effort, even as casualties mounted and victory seemed increasingly elusive.

McCarthy's entry into the race followed months of unsuccessful efforts to persuade other prominent Democrats to challenge Johnson. Robert Kennedy, the most obvious anti-war standard-bearer, had declined to run, fearing that a challenge to Johnson would be seen as a personal vendetta rather than principled opposition. Senator George McGovern of South Dakota had also demurred, as had Senator Frank Church of Idaho.

The decision fell to McCarthy almost by default. At a November 1967 meeting with anti-war activists, the Minnesota senator agreed to make the race, but with characteristic understatement. "I'm prepared to go as far as anyone wants to go," he said quietly. It was hardly the stuff of revolutionary manifestos, but it was enough.

What transformed McCarthy's cerebral candidacy into a political phenomenon was the energy of young Americans who saw his campaign as their vehicle for ending an increasingly unpopular war. College students began arriving in New Hampshire as early as December 1967, drawn by word-of-mouth networks and underground newspapers that portrayed McCarthy as the only politician willing to challenge the war machine.

These volunteers brought assets that conventional political campaigns had never possessed: unlimited time, idealistic energy, and a willingness to work for free. They also brought liabilities that horrified traditional campaign managers: long hair, unconventional dress, and political views that extended far beyond opposition to Vietnam to encompass broader challenges to American foreign policy and domestic institutions.

The solution, devised by McCarthy's young campaign coordinators, was as simple as it was effective: "Get Clean for Gene." Student volunteers would cut their hair, don conservative clothing, and present themselves as clean-cut college students rather than anti-war protesters. The transformation was remarkable—and strategically brilliant.

"We took the most radical message in American politics and packaged it in the most conservative possible presentation," recalled Sam Brown, one of McCarthy's student coordinators. "We weren't hippies or radicals—we were your sons and daughters, home from college to save the country."

This army of student volunteers compensated for McCarthy's organizational and financial disadvantages through sheer numbers and dedication. They knocked on doors throughout New Hampshire's small towns and rural areas, places where presidential candidates rarely ventured and where opposition to the war ran deeper than most politicians realized. They distributed literature, made phone calls, and engaged in the kind of personal conversations that could change minds—and votes.

The contrast with Johnson's campaign could not have been more striking. The president, confident of an easy victory, barely campaigned in New Hampshire. His organization relied on traditional Democratic party structures and endorsed candidates, assuming that party loyalty would triumph over anti-war sentiment. They fundamentally misunderstood how the war had altered the political landscape.

McCarthy's breakthrough in New Hampshire cannot be understood without reference to the Tet Offensive. This massive North Vietnamese and Viet Cong attack began on January 30, 1968, just weeks before the New Hampshire primary. Although American and South Vietnamese forces ultimately repelled the attacks, the psychological impact was devastating. For three years, the Johnson administration had assured Americans that victory in Vietnam was imminent. Tet made such claims appear delusional.

The offensive transformed the political context of McCarthy's campaign overnight. What had begun as a protest candidacy appealing primarily to committed anti-war activists suddenly resonated with mainstream voters who were simply tired of an endless, inconclusive conflict. McCarthy's message evolved from moral opposition to the war to pragmatic skepticism about the administration's competence.

"The issue isn't whether you support or oppose the war," McCarthy told audiences in New Hampshire's final weeks. "The issue is whether you believe this administration knows how to end it." This subtle shift in emphasis broadened his appeal beyond the anti-war movement to include voters who supported American objectives in Vietnam but doubted Johnson's ability to achieve them.

The Tet Offensive also provided McCarthy with credibility that his previous Senate record had not established. For months, he had argued that the war was unwinnable and that administration officials were misleading the American people about progress in Vietnam. Tet appeared to vindicate these claims, transforming McCarthy from a fringe critic into a prophetic voice who had seen through official deceptions.

Television coverage of the Tet fighting reinforced McCarthy's message in ways that no campaign advertisement could have achieved. Night after night, Americans watched bloody street fighting in cities that the administration had claimed were secure. The disconnect between official optimism and televised reality created exactly the credibility gap that McCarthy had been highlighting for months.

The transformation of McCarthy's candidacy from curiosity to phenomenon owed much to the national media's growing fascination with his student volunteers and their apparent success in connecting with New Hampshire voters. Television producers, always hungry for compelling visuals, found the story of college students abandoning their studies to campaign for peace in small New England towns.

The coverage took on mythic proportions. Network correspondents filed daily reports about the "Children's Crusade," emphasizing the generational divide between McCarthy's young volunteers and Johnson's older supporters. Newspapers ran feature stories about students sleeping on gymnasium floors and surviving on peanut butter sandwiches while they canvassed for their candidate.

This media attention created a feedback loop that strengthened McCarthy's campaign in unexpected ways. The coverage attracted additional volunteers, drawn by the romantic notion of participating in a historic political movement. It also provided McCarthy with free publicity that his underfunded campaign could never have afforded through paid advertising.

More importantly, the extensive media coverage forced New Hampshire voters to take McCarthy's candidacy seriously. What might have remained a marginal protest campaign gained legitimacy through the simple fact of sustained national attention. Voters who had never heard of Eugene McCarthy learned about his campaign through television reports about his remarkable volunteers.

The media narrative also played to New Hampshire's political culture, which prized the state's first-in-the-nation primary status and took seriously the responsibility of vetting presidential candidates. New Hampshire voters, aware that the nation was watching their judgment, were more willing to consider an unconventional candidate than they might have been in a less visible contest.

As McCarthy's poll numbers began climbing in New Hampshire's final weeks, the Johnson administration mounted an increasingly desperate counterattack. Administration officials flooded the state with surrogates who warned that a vote for McCarthy was a vote for American defeat in Vietnam. They argued that challenging a sitting president during wartime was unpatriotic and would encourage America's enemies.

The counterattack revealed the establishment's fundamental misunderstanding of the political moment. Johnson's supporters assumed that traditional appeals to party loyalty and patriotic duty would trump voter dissatisfaction with the war. They failed to recognize how completely the political landscape had shifted since Tet.

Secretary of Agriculture Orville Freeman, a former Minnesota governor who had known McCarthy for decades, campaigned throughout New Hampshire, warning that his fellow Minnesotan was a "dangerous radical" whose victory would "encourage the Communists in Hanoi." The message backfired, making McCarthy appear more significant than his poll numbers suggested while reinforcing his image as a truth-teller willing to challenge official orthodoxy.

Even more damaging to Johnson was the administration's tendency to dismiss McCarthy's student volunteers as unrepresentative extremists. This characterization might have worked against a candidate supported primarily by long-haired protesters. Still, it seemed absurd when applied to the clean-cut college students who were knocking on doors throughout New Hampshire.

"They keep calling our volunteers radicals," McCarthy observed wryly during a February campaign stop. "Have you seen them? They look like they're running for student body president." The line always drew laughter, but it also made a serious point about the administration's disconnect from political reality.

When New Hampshire voters went to the polls on March 12, 1968, few observers expected anything more than a respectable showing for McCarthy. The most optimistic projections gave him perhaps 25 percent of the vote—enough to claim moral victory but not enough to fundamentally alter the presidential race.

The actual results stunned the political world. McCarthy won 42 percent of the vote to Johnson's 49 percent, a margin so narrow that it constituted a devastating psychological defeat for the sitting president. More importantly, when write-in votes and delegate allocations were calculated, McCarthy had actually won more New Hampshire delegates than Johnson—a technical victory that amplified the political impact of his strong showing.

The numbers told only part of the story. Exit polls revealed that McCarthy had not merely consolidated the anti-war vote but had attracted significant support from voters concerned about the economy, domestic unrest, and the administration's general competence. He had run strongly across demographic lines, winning among both young and elderly voters, in both urban and rural areas.

The immediate political consequences were dramatic. Within hours of the New Hampshire results, Robert Kennedy announced that he was "reassessing" his decision not to challenge Johnson. Republican commentators, who had assumed they would face a weakened but renominated Johnson in November, began preparing for a contested Democratic convention and an uncertain general election opponent.

Most significantly, the New Hampshire results established McCarthy as a legitimate contender rather than a protest candidate. His campaign, which had struggled to raise money and attract experienced staff, suddenly found itself flooded with volunteers, donations, and endorsements from Democratic officials who had previously dismissed his candidacy.

Yet even as McCarthy's New Hampshire breakthrough shocked the political establishment, it revealed the limitations that would ultimately prevent him from sustaining his success. His appeal remained concentrated among educated, affluent voters who opposed the war on moral or intellectual grounds. He had made little progress with the working-class Democrats, African Americans, and ethnic voters who formed the party's base.

More problematically, McCarthy's cerebral style and anti-political persona, which had served him well in New Hampshire's intimate retail politics, proved less effective in larger, more diverse primary states. His reluctance to engage in traditional political activities—fundraising dinners, endorsement meetings, coalition-building sessions—limited his ability to build the broad organizational support necessary for a sustained campaign.

The New Hampshire breakthrough also attracted Robert Kennedy into the race, setting up a competition for anti-war votes that would ultimately benefit neither candidate. Kennedy's entry fragmented the anti-war movement and created bitter divisions within the Democratic Party that would persist long after the 1968 election.

Perhaps most importantly, McCarthy's breakthrough revealed the difference between leading a movement and leading a party. His campaign had successfully mobilized anti-war sentiment and demonstrated the depth of dissatisfaction with Johnson's policies. But movements and political parties operate according to different logics, requiring different skills and appealing to different constituencies.

Despite its ultimate failure to secure the nomination, McCarthy's New Hampshire breakthrough fundamentally altered American presidential politics. It demonstrated that sitting presidents were not invulnerable to primary challenges, encouraging future insurgent candidacies from Ted Kennedy in 1980 to Pat Buchanan in 1992. It showed that single-issue campaigns could achieve remarkable success if they tapped into deep voter dissatisfaction.

Most importantly, McCarthy's breakthrough established the template for insurgent campaigns that would follow: mobilize passionate activists, present a clear alternative to establishment policies, generate free media coverage through unconventional tactics, and hope to create momentum that could overcome organizational and financial disadvantages.

The "Children's Crusade" also pioneered the use of young volunteers as a campaign resource, demonstrating that idealistic energy could substitute for traditional political assets. Every subsequent insurgent campaign—from McGovern in 1972 to Obama in 2008—would attempt to replicate McCarthy's success in mobilizing young activists.

By forcing Lyndon Johnson from the presidential race—Johnson announced his withdrawal on March 31, less than three weeks after New Hampshire—McCarthy achieved something unprecedented in American politics. He had used the primary system to end a presidency, proving that in the television age, a single breakthrough moment could have consequences that resonated far beyond the confines of electoral politics.

The poet warrior had done something that all the generals, all the pundits, and all the party leaders had failed to accomplish: he had found a way to make democracy work, even against the most powerful political figure in the world. It was a breakthrough that would inspire generations of political insurgents, even as it demonstrated the enormous gulf between capturing lightning in a bottle and sustaining it long enough to reach the White House.

Lessons for Modern Candidates

McCarthy's New Hampshire shock offers three crucial insights for contemporary insurgent candidates seeking to challenge established frontrunners.

First, external events can transform political landscapes overnight. The Tet Offensive gave credibility to arguments McCarthy had been making for months, turning him from a fringe critic into a prophetic voice. Modern candidates should prepare to capitalize on "black swan" events that vindicate their positions, whether economic crises, foreign policy failures, or social upheavals. The key is having a consistent message that can be reframed rather than fundamentally altered when circumstances change.

Second, presentation matters as much as the message. The "Get Clean for Gene" strategy revealed the critical importance of packaging radical ideas in mainstream terms. McCarthy's volunteers looked like mainstream America even as they advocated for fundamental policy change. Today's insurgent candidates must similarly ensure that their appearance and presentation don't overshadow their message—Alexandria Ocasio-Cortez's success owes much to her ability to advocate for progressive policies while maintaining an accessible, relatable persona.

Third, volunteer energy has both power and limitations. Student activists provided unprecedented ground-level organization, but couldn't substitute for traditional coalition-building. Modern insurgent campaigns must learn to harness grassroots enthusiasm while simultaneously building relationships with established political actors. Obama's 2008 campaign succeeded where McCarthy's failed partly because it combined grassroots organizing with systematic outreach to party leaders and institutional players.

The McCarthy breakthrough established the template for modern insurgent politics: seize on external events that vindicate your message, package that message for mainstream consumption, and mobilize passionate volunteers to overcome resource disadvantages. But his ultimate failure serves as an equally important lesson: breakthrough moments must evolve into sustainable coalitions, or they risk being co-opted by more traditional politicians who better understand the complex demands of party politics.

“McGovern’s insurgency demonstrated both the potential and the limitations of breakthrough politics in the modern primary system.”

3

MCGOVERN INSURGENCY (1972)

The letter arrived at George McGovern's Senate office on a gray February morning in 1971, buried among the usual stack of constituent mail and legislative correspondence. It was from a college student in Colorado who had never met the South Dakota senator but had heard him speak against the Vietnam War. "Senator McGovern," the young man wrote, "you may be the only person in Washington who understands that this war is destroying our country. Please don't let us down."

McGovern's aide, Jeff Smith, found his boss staring at the letter long after he had finished reading it. "How many more of these have we received?" McGovern asked quietly.

"About two thousand this month," Smith replied. "All saying pretty much the same thing."

It was then that McGovern understood something that the political establishment in Washington had completely missed: the anti-war sentiment that had driven Eugene McCarthy's breakthrough in 1968 had not dissipated with Richard Nixon's election—it had deepened, broadened, and was searching for a new champion. The question was whether the mild-mannered former history professor from South Dakota could transform that sentiment into a political victory.

By the time McGovern accepted the Democratic nomination in Miami Beach on July 13, 1972, he had accomplished something that political scientists considered nearly impossible: he had captured his party's presidential nomination despite starting the race with less than 2 percent support in national polls and virtually no endorsements from Democratic leaders. His insurgency represented the ultimate triumph of movement politics over establishment control, but it would also reveal the devastating consequences when breakthrough energy cannot be translated into broad electoral appeal.

George McGovern seemed as unlikely a revolutionary as Eugene McCarthy had four years earlier, but for different reasons. Where McCarthy was intellectual and detached, McGovern was earnest and moralistic. Where McCarthy attracted sophisticated college students with his poetry and philosophical approach to politics, McGovern appealed to activists through his unwavering commitment to ending the Vietnam War and expanding social justice.

The son of a Methodist minister from small-town South Dakota, McGovern had built his political career on prairie populism and moral conviction rather than charisma or political cunning. His Senate colleagues respected his sincerity and expertise on agricultural issues but considered him too liberal and too plain-spoken for national politics. Even his supporters acknowledged that he lacked the political instincts that seemed essential for presidential success.

"George was the most honest politician I ever met," recalled Gary Hart, who served as McGovern's campaign manager. "Unfortunately, that wasn't necessarily an advantage in presidential politics."

McGovern's decision to seek the presidency grew directly from his frustration with the Democratic Party's failure to end the Vietnam War after winning control of Congress in 1970. Unlike McCarthy, whose anti-war stance had been primarily moral and intellectual, McGovern's opposition was deeply personal. He had served as a bomber pilot in World War II and understood the difference between necessary and unnecessary wars. Vietnam, in his view, was not only wrong but also a betrayal of everything America should represent.

This moral clarity gave McGovern's candidacy a sense of mission that was often lacking in conventional political campaigns. His supporters weren't just backing a candidate—they were joining a crusade to reclaim American values from what they saw as a corrupt and militaristic establishment. It was exactly the kind of message that could inspire passionate activism, but might struggle to attract mainstream voters.

What transformed McGovern from a fringe candidate into a potential nominee was his role in rewriting the Democratic Party's nomination rules following the disaster of the 1968 Chicago convention. As chairman of the Commission on Party Structure and Delegate Selection—known universally as the McGovern-Fraser Commission—he had helped design reforms that would revolutionize presidential politics.

The new rules required state parties to provide "meaningful participation" for women, minorities, and young people in the delegate selection process. They mandated that delegates be chosen through open processes like primaries or open caucuses rather than closed party meetings. Most importantly, they shifted power from party leaders to activists and primary voters, creating exactly the kind of system that favored insurgent candidates like McGovern.

"We didn't set out to help my presidential campaign," McGovern later claimed, but the rules changes clearly benefited candidates who could mobilize passionate supporters and navigate complex delegate selection processes. Traditional political assets—endorsements from party leaders, support from labor unions, fundraising connections with major donors—became less important than the ability to organize committed activists in dozens of states simultaneously.

The irony was delicious: McGovern had helped create the very system that made his own breakthrough possible. While establishment candidates like Edmund Muskie and Hubert Humphrey continued to campaign as if the old rules still applied, McGovern's organization was perfectly positioned to exploit the new delegate selection landscape.

"The other candidates were playing checkers while we were playing chess," observed Frank Mankiewicz, McGovern's political director. "They were focused on winning primaries, while we were focused on winning delegates."

McGovern's breakthrough required more than favorable rules—it needed a perfect storm of circumstances that would create opportunities for an insurgent campaign. That storm materialized in early 1972 through a series of events that nobody could have predicted, but that McGovern's campaign was uniquely positioned to exploit.

The first element was the collapse of Edmund Muskie's front-running campaign. The Maine senator had entered the race as the overwhelming favorite, endorsed by most Democratic leaders and blessed with the kind of centrist appeal that seemed ideal for challenging Nixon. But Muskie's campaign proved brittle under pressure, most notably when he appeared to cry while defending his wife against attacks in a New Hampshire newspaper. The moment of perceived weakness destroyed his image as a steady alternative to Nixon and opened space for other candidates.

The second element was the entry of Alabama Governor George Wallace, whose segregationist appeal drew conservative Democratic voters away from mainstream candidates and allowed McGovern to win primaries with pluralities rather than majorities. Wallace's presence in the race created a three-way split in many states that favored whoever could most effectively mobilize their core supporters, exactly McGovern's strength.

The third element was the shooting of Wallace in Maryland, which removed him from active campaigning just as the primary season was entering its crucial final phase. Wallace's supporters, suddenly without their preferred candidate, were up for grabs, but most establishment Democrats found their views too extreme to court. McGovern, meanwhile, could focus entirely on consolidating the liberal vote.

Finally, the new campaign finance laws that took effect in 1972 created an environment that favored candidates who could attract small-dollar contributions from passionate supporters. McGovern's anti-war message proved enormously effective at generating donations through direct mail, allowing his campaign to remain competitive financially even without major donor support.

McGovern's breakthrough moment came in Wisconsin on April 4, 1972, when he scored a decisive victory that established him as the principal alternative to the collapsing establishment candidates. With 30 percent of the vote, McGovern finished well ahead of Wallace (22 percent), Humphrey (21 percent), and Muskie (10 percent), demonstrating that an anti-war liberal could win in a blue-collar, industrial state.

The Wisconsin victory was remarkable not just for its margin but for its composition. Exit polls showed that McGovern had assembled a coalition that extended beyond the college-educated, affluent liberals who formed his core support. He had won significant support from working-class voters who opposed the war, from African Americans who appreciated his civil rights record, and from women who were drawn to his campaign's emphasis on gender equality.

"Wisconsin proved that we weren't just a boutique campaign for suburban liberals," recalled Hart. "We had put together a coalition that could compete in industrial states against traditional Democratic politicians."

The victory also demonstrated the effectiveness of McGovern's grassroots organizing approach. While other campaigns relied heavily on paid advertising and endorsements from local politicians, McGovern's volunteers had spent months building relationships with activists, union dissidents, and community leaders. This ground-up approach proved particularly effective in Wisconsin's tradition of progressive politics.

Media coverage of the Wisconsin primary reinforced McGovern's emerging narrative as the candidate of change and idealism. Television reporters contrasted his enthusiastic young volunteers with the tired-looking professionals working for establishment candidates. Newspaper columnists wrote admiringly about his detailed policy proposals and his willingness to take controversial stands on issues like defense spending and tax reform.

What truly distinguished McGovern's 1972 campaign was its sophisticated understanding of the complex delegate selection process that would ultimately determine the nomination. While most campaigns focused on winning primaries and generating favorable media coverage, McGovern's organization was simultaneously engaged in the less glamorous but more decisive work of accumulating convention delegates.

This "delegate hunt" required a different set of skills than traditional campaigning. Instead of appealing to broad audiences through television and rallies, McGovern's operatives needed to identify and mobilize the small numbers of activists who would actually participate in caucuses and convention processes. They needed to understand arcane party rules and master parliamentary procedures. Most importantly, they needed to sustain their organizing efforts over many months, long after media attention had moved on to other stories.

McGovern's campaign excelled at this unglamorous work because it was staffed by activists who understood movement politics. Many of his key organizers had cut their teeth in the civil rights movement, the anti-war movement, or the emerging women's movement. They brought skills in grassroots organizing that conventional political operatives often lacked.

"We treated every state like a separate campaign," explained Rick Stearns, McGovern's delegate coordinator and later a federal judge. "We had detailed plans for accumulating delegates in states that other campaigns had written off."

This attention to delegate mathematics became crucial as the primary season progressed. McGovern rarely won outright majorities in contested primaries, but his superior organization allowed him to maximize his delegate haul in each state. In Pennsylvania, for example, he finished third in the popular vote but won more delegates than any other candidate by understanding the state's complex district-by-district allocation rules.

As McGovern's delegate lead became apparent in late spring 1972, the Democratic establishment mounted an increasingly desperate counterattack designed to deny him the nomination. Party leaders who had largely ignored his candidacy suddenly awakened to the possibility that their party might nominate someone they considered an extremist who would lead Democrats to catastrophic defeat.

The "Stop McGovern" movement took several forms. Labor leaders, led by AFL-CIO president George Meany, publicly denounced McGovern's liberal positions and threatened to withhold support from his general election campaign. Southern Democratic governors warned that McGovern's civil rights positions would cost the party the South for a generation. Even liberal Democrats like Mayor John Lindsay of New York expressed private concerns about McGovern's electability.

More concretely, establishment figures attempted to recruit alternative candidates who could unite the party's mainstream. Hubert Humphrey, despite his weak primary showing, was encouraged to remain in the race as a potential compromise choice. Senator Henry Jackson of Washington was promoted as a more moderate alternative on defense issues. There was even brief speculation about drafting Senator Ted Kennedy, despite his repeated insistence that he would not run.

The counterattack reached its climax at the California primary on June 6, 1972, when Humphrey launched a series of increasingly sharp attacks on McGovern's positions. In a televised debate, Humphrey accused McGovern of proposing "giveaway programs" that would bankrupt the federal government and characterized his defense positions as naive and dangerous.

McGovern's response revealed both his strengths and weaknesses as a candidate. He defended his positions with moral passion and intellectual precision, but seemed genuinely hurt by attacks from a fellow liberal. "I can't believe Hubert is saying these things," he confided to aides after one particularly brutal exchange.

McGovern's 44 percent victory in California on June 6 effectively secured his nomination by giving him a commanding lead in delegates and demonstrating his ability to win in the nation's largest state. The victory was particularly impressive because it came despite intense negative campaigning from Humphrey and massive spending by establishment-backed opponents.

The California results also revealed the breadth of McGovern's coalition, which had expanded far beyond its original base of anti-war activists and college-educated liberals. Exit polls showed significant support from Chicano voters drawn to his positions on immigration and civil rights, from environmentalists attracted to his conservation proposals, and from working-class voters who appreciated his populist economic message.

"California proved that we had built a majority coalition within the Democratic Party," McGovern declared in his victory speech. "We represent the future of American politics."

Yet even as McGovern celebrated his breakthrough to the nomination, warning signs were already apparent. His victory margin in California was smaller than expected, and his coalition remained heavily concentrated among the most liberal Democrats. Moderate and conservative Democrats, who would be essential for a general election victory, remained skeptical of his candidacy.

More ominously, polls showed McGovern trailing Nixon by enormous margins among general election voters. His positions on issues like defense spending, welfare reform, and social issues appealed strongly to Democratic activists but seemed out of step with mainstream American opinion.

McGovern's breakthrough culminated in his nomination at the Democratic National Convention in Miami Beach. Still, the convention also revealed the challenges he would face in translating primary success into a general election victory. His acceptance speech, delivered at 2:48 AM Eastern time due to convention delays, reached a much smaller television audience than anticipated. The speech itself, while eloquent, emphasized themes of moral reform and social justice that resonated with delegates but might not appeal to swing voters.

More problematically, the convention showcased the very liberal activists who had powered McGovern's breakthrough but who reinforced his image as the candidate of the far left. Television cameras captured delegates who looked and sounded very different from typical American voters: young, affluent, highly educated, and passionate about issues like feminism and environmentalism that remained controversial with many Americans.

"We looked like we were nominating the candidate of NPR and the faculty lounge," one McGovern adviser later reflected ruefully. "It was great for energizing our base, but terrible for appealing to the middle-class voters we needed in November."

The delegate composition reflected the success of McGovern's breakthrough but also its limitations. The new party rules he had helped design had indeed opened the process to women, minorities, and young people—but at the expense of the white working-class voters, union members, and ethnic Democrats who had traditionally formed the party's backbone.

McGovern's insurgency demonstrated both the potential and the limitations of breakthrough politics in the modern primary system. His campaign had successfully exploited new rules, new technologies, and new constituencies to overcome enormous institutional disadvantages. He had proven that passionate activists could triumph over establishment opposition and that moral conviction could substitute for traditional political assets.

Yet McGovern's breakthrough also revealed why insurgent campaigns often struggle to transition from primary success to general election victory. The very qualities that enabled his breakthrough—ideological purity, activist energy, and moral certainty—made it difficult for him to appeal to the broad center of American politics.

The coalition that carried McGovern to the nomination was too narrow and too liberal for general election success. His positions on issues like defense spending, welfare policy, and social issues might energize Democratic activists but alienate the moderate voters who typically determine presidential elections. His campaign organization, built around grassroots activism and moral suasion, lacked the professional competence needed for a national general election campaign.

Most fundamentally, McGovern never solved the challenge that confronts all breakthrough candidates: how to maintain the energy and authenticity that drove their initial success while broadening their appeal sufficiently to win over skeptical voters. His attempts to moderate his positions or emphasize his mainstream credentials seemed inauthentic and confused his core supporters without attracting new ones.

The limitations of McGovern's breakthrough became apparent on November 7, 1972, when he suffered one of the most devastating defeats in presidential history, losing to Nixon by 23 percentage points and carrying only Massachusetts and the District of Columbia. The defeat was so comprehensive that it seemed to vindicate every criticism that establishment Democrats had made about his candidacy.

Exit polls revealed the narrowness of McGovern's appeal. He had lost not only conservative and moderate Republicans, as expected, but also significant numbers of traditionally Democratic voters. White working-class voters, who had been the backbone of Democratic presidential coalitions since the New Deal, abandoned the party in massive numbers. Even many liberal voters who agreed with McGovern's positions on the war and social issues found him unpresidential or incompetent.

The defeat had consequences that extended far beyond McGovern's personal political fortunes. It convinced many Democrats that liberal insurgencies were electoral suicide and that the party needed to move toward the center to remain competitive. It also demonstrated to Republican strategists that Democrats could be successfully portrayed as the party of cultural elites and radical social change.

Despite its ultimate failure, McGovern's insurgency left a lasting impact on American presidential politics. It proved that the reformed primary system could produce nominees who were dramatically different from traditional political figures. It demonstrated the power of grassroots organizing, direct mail fundraising, and issue-based activism in presidential campaigns.

Most importantly, McGovern's breakthrough established a template for liberal insurgencies that would influence Democratic politics for decades. His emphasis on expanding participation, challenging establishment orthodoxy, and organizing passionate activists would be echoed in later campaigns from Jesse Jackson to Howard Dean to Bernie Sanders.

The McGovern insurgency also revealed the fundamental tension between breakthrough and sustainability that defines modern presidential politics. McGovern had mastered the art of breaking through—of capturing attention, mobilizing supporters, and disrupting establishment expectations. But he never solved the challenge of translation—converting breakthrough energy into broad political appeal.

"George McGovern showed that anyone could win the Democratic nomination if they understood the rules and organized effectively," reflected Hart years later. "What he couldn't show was how to win the presidency once you got the nomination."

The prairie populist had achieved something remarkable: he had taken a party's presidential nomination despite starting with virtually no institutional support. But in doing so, he had also demonstrated the limitations of purely insurgent politics and the enormous gulf between leading a movement and leading a nation. His breakthrough would inspire generations of liberal activists, even as his defeat would haunt Democratic strategists for decades to come.

Lessons for Modern Candidates

McGovern's 1972 insurgency offers three crucial insights for contemporary candidates seeking to transform grassroots movements into electoral success.

First, master the rules while others ignore them. McGovern's role in rewriting the Democratic Party's delegate selection rules gave him an enormous strategic advantage—he understood the new system while establishment candidates continued operating under old assumptions. Modern insurgents must similarly invest in understanding campaign finance laws, delegate allocation formulas, and ballot access requirements that mainstream candidates take for granted. Bernie Sanders' success in accumulating delegates despite losing key primaries in 2016 and 2020 reflected this same systematic approach to the rules of the game.

Second, build coalitions beyond your base early, not late. McGovern's breakthrough was powered by passionate activists who shared his liberal worldview, but this narrow coalition proved insufficient for general election success. Contemporary insurgent candidates must begin broadening their appeal while still in primary mode, rather than attempting to pivot after securing the nomination. Obama's 2008 campaign succeeded partly because it simultaneously energized progressive activists and courted moderate Democrats, union leaders, and even some Republicans from the beginning.

Third, organize for delegates, not just headlines. McGovern's campaign excelled at the unglamorous work of accumulating convention delegates through superior organization and attention to complex state-by-state rules. While media coverage focused on primary victories and poll numbers, McGovern's team was methodically building an insurmountable delegate lead. Modern candidates must similarly balance the need for favorable media coverage with the mathematical realities of delegate accumulation, understanding that winning the nomination requires delegates, not just momentum.

McGovern's breakthrough demonstrated that passionate movements can capture major party nominations when they combine ideological clarity with organizational sophistication. But his catastrophic general election defeat serves as an equally important lesson: insurgent energy must be translated into broader appeal, or breakthrough victories become pyrrhic triumphs. The prairie populist proved that anyone could win a party's nomination with enough dedication and tactical skill—but also that nominations are just the beginning, not the end, of the quest for political power.

"Carter's systematic approach to primary campaigning and his emphasis on personal authenticity would be emulated by future insurgent candidates."

4

CARTER MIRACLE (1976)

The question came from a reporter in the back of the room at the National Press Club in Washington, delivered with the kind of barely concealed smirk that political journalists reserved for candidates they considered unserious. It was December 1974, and Jimmy Carter had just finished outlining his intention to seek the presidency to an audience of perhaps thirty people, most of whom seemed more interested in their lunch than in the former governor of Georgia.

"Governor Carter," the reporter asked, "can you tell us exactly who you are? I mean, Jimmy who?"

Carter smiled with the patience of a Sunday school teacher addressing a particularly slow student. "My name is Jimmy Carter," he said slowly, "and I'm going to be the next president of the United States."

The room erupted in barely suppressed laughter. Here was a one-term governor from Georgia—a state that had never produced a president—with no Washington experience, no national organization, and no recognition outside the South, claiming he would defeat a field that included senators, governors, and nationally known figures. It seemed like the most preposterous political boast since Harold Stassen had announced his latest presidential campaign.

Twenty months later, on July 15, 1976, Jimmy Carter accepted the Democratic nomination for president at Madison Square Garden, having accomplished perhaps the most improbable breakthrough in modern political history. Starting from complete obscurity and with virtually no institutional support, he had navigated the complex landscape of post-reform Democratic politics to capture his party's highest honor. His victory would demonstrate that in the new primary system, outsider status could be transformed from a liability into the ultimate political asset—if the candidate possessed the strategic vision and tactical discipline to exploit the changing rules of presidential politics.

Jimmy Carter's decision to seek the presidency grew from a cold-eyed analysis of how the post-McGovern reforms had altered the path to the Democratic nomination. Where other potential candidates saw the proliferation of primaries as a burden—expensive, time-consuming contests that favored celebrities and demagogues—Carter recognized them as an opportunity for someone willing to make the total commitment that his better-known rivals could not or would not make.

The calculation was elegantly simple: if the nomination now required winning primaries rather than courting party leaders, then the candidate who started earliest, worked hardest, and understood the new rules most thoroughly would possess decisive advantages over more prominent figures who relied on traditional political assets. Carter's obscurity, rather than being a fatal weakness, could become a strength if he could use the primary process to introduce himself to voters on his terms.

"The other candidates had to protect their existing positions," recalled Hamilton Jordan, Carter's brilliant young campaign manager. "Jimmy had nothing to lose and everything to gain. That gave us a freedom that none of our competitors possessed."

This strategic insight led Carter to make a commitment that his rivals initially considered absurd: he would campaign full-time for the presidency for two solid years, visiting every early primary state multiple times and building personal relationships with the activists and local leaders who would ultimately determine the outcome. While senators like Henry Jackson and Birch Bayh remained in Washington tending to their legislative duties, Carter was shaking hands in Iowa coffee shops and New Hampshire diners.

The approach reflected Carter's background as a businessman and engineer who believed that most problems could be solved through careful planning and systematic effort. He applied the same methodical approach to presidential politics that he had used to modernize his family's peanut business and reform Georgia's state government. If winning required visiting 200 towns in Iowa, he would visit 200 towns. If success demanded memorizing the names of 500 local Democratic officials, he would memorize 500 names.

Carter's breakthrough began in Iowa, where his campaign recognized an opportunity that other candidates had largely ignored. The Iowa caucuses, scheduled for January 19, 1976, would be the first formal contest of the presidential season, but most campaigns treated them as a minor warm-up event before the more important New Hampshire primary. Iowa was considered too small, too rural, and too unrepresentative to significantly influence the national race.

Carter saw Iowa differently. As a former governor of a rural southern state, he understood agricultural issues and could speak naturally to farming communities. More importantly, Iowa's caucus system rewarded exactly the kind of intensive personal campaigning at which Carter excelled. Success required identifying supporters and ensuring they actually attended their neighborhood caucuses—a process that favored organization and personal relationships over name recognition and paid advertising.

Carter's Iowa strategy began almost two years before the caucuses, with visits to small towns throughout the state where he would spend entire days meeting voters one-on-one. He would arrive in a community early in the morning, visit the local diner for breakfast, tour a farm or small business, attend a coffee hour at someone's home, speak to a service club at lunch, and end the day at a potluck dinner with local Democrats. By the time he left, he would have met dozens of people personally and collected hundreds of names for his growing Iowa database.

"Jimmy understood that Iowa voters expected to know their candidates personally," explained Tim Kraft, Carter's Iowa coordinator. "He was willing to make that investment in a way that other candidates weren't."

This intensive courtship paid dividends in ways that went beyond vote totals. Local Democratic activists became unpaid Carter organizers, recommending him to friends and neighbors with the kind of personal endorsement that no amount of advertising could purchase. Newspaper editors in small Iowa towns, impressed by Carter's willingness to visit their communities, wrote favorable columns that helped establish his credibility with their readers.

The approach also generated the kind of authentic moments that would become central to Carter's political appeal. Stories circulated throughout Iowa about the governor who had helped a farmer fix his tractor, who had stayed up late discussing foreign policy with a group of college students, who had remembered the names of voters' children from previous visits. These anecdotes, spreading through word-of-mouth networks, created an image of Carter as genuinely different from typical politicians.

What transformed Carter's systematic approach to campaigning into a political breakthrough was his ability to package methodical preparation as spontaneous authenticity. At a time when voters were deeply cynical about politicians following the Watergate scandal and the Vietnam War, Carter presented himself as a different kind of candidate—honest, moral, and uncontaminated by the corruption of Washington politics.

This authentic brand was both genuine and carefully constructed. Carter's religious faith was real and deep, but his campaign skillfully emphasized it in ways that appealed to voters seeking moral leadership. His outsider status was an unavoidable fact, but his advisers transformed it into evidence of his independence from special interests and establishment thinking. His detailed policy knowledge was the product of intensive briefings, but he presented it as the natural wisdom of someone unencumbered by Washington groupthink.

The "I'll never lie to you" promise that became Carter's signature line exemplified this blend of authentic conviction and strategic calculation. The promise reflected Carter's genuine commitment to truthfulness, but it also served as an implicit critique of the Nixon administration's deceptions and the broader culture of political dishonesty that Watergate had revealed. Voters heard both the personal commitment and the political message.

Carter's authenticity brand was reinforced by seemingly spontaneous moments that were actually the product of careful advance work. His decision to carry his own luggage generated photographs that conveyed humility and frugality. His stays in supporters' homes rather than hotels created stories about a candidate who lived like ordinary Americans. His willingness to answer any question, no matter how difficult, suggested a transparency that contrasted sharply with the evasiveness of typical politicians.

"Everything Jimmy did was authentic, but we also made sure that his authenticity was visible," acknowledged Jody Powell, Carter's press secretary. "We understood that being genuine wasn't enough—you had to communicate your genuineness effectively."

Carter's Iowa breakthrough on January 19, 1976, exceeded even his campaign's optimistic projections. With 28 percent of the vote, he finished well ahead of his nearest competitors and demonstrated that an unknown southerner could compete successfully in the Midwest. The victory generated precisely the kind of national media attention that Carter needed to become a credible candidate in other states.

But Iowa alone could not sustain a presidential campaign. Carter needed to prove that his appeal extended beyond rural, agricultural communities to the more diverse electorate that would determine the Democratic nomination. New Hampshire, with its tradition of independent-minded voters and retail politics, provided the perfect opportunity for Carter to validate his Iowa breakthrough.

The New Hampshire campaign revealed Carter's ability to adapt his message and style to different political environments while maintaining his core appeal as an authentic outsider. Where his Iowa campaign had emphasized agricultural issues and small-town values, his New Hampshire effort focused on government reform and fiscal responsibility—themes that resonated with the state's traditionally conservative Democrats and independent voters.

Carter's New Hampshire organization, built around the same intensive personal campaigning that had succeeded in Iowa, proved equally effective in a different political culture. He visited paper mills and defense plants, attended town halls and coffee hours, and walked main streets in dozens of New Hampshire communities. By primary day, he had personally met an estimated 20,000 New Hampshire voters—an extraordinary achievement in a state with fewer than 100,000 Democratic primary voters.

The February 24 New Hampshire primary delivered the validation that Carter needed. His 28 percent victory margin, achieved against a field that included several better-known candidates, established him as the clear Democratic frontrunner and generated a wave of media coverage that transformed his national profile overnight. Time and Newsweek featured him on their covers. Network television news programs profiled his family and his small-town Georgia roots. Suddenly, Jimmy Carter was no longer "Jimmy who?"

What distinguished Carter's 1976 breakthrough from previous insurgent campaigns was his ability to transform early victories into sustained momentum. Where other breakthrough candidates had struggled to capitalize on their initial success, Carter's campaign had developed a systematic approach to leveraging primary wins into organizational and financial advantages in subsequent contests.

The key was Carter's understanding of the new realities of primary politics. In the reformed system, winning early primaries generated media coverage that improved name recognition, which made fundraising easier, which allowed for expanded campaigning, which increased the chances of winning later primaries. Success bred success, but only if campaigns were organized to exploit the momentum that victories created.

Carter's campaign had prepared for this momentum phase by identifying key activists and potential supporters in every primary state months before the contests began. When the Iowa and New Hampshire victories generated national attention, these pre-identified contacts became the foundation for rapid organizational expansion. Local Democratic leaders who had been lukewarm about Carter suddenly returned his campaign's phone calls. Fundraisers who had previously ignored his solicitations began organizing events. Volunteers who had been waiting to see if he was viable suddenly committed to his campaign.

"We didn't just win Iowa and New Hampshire," explained Jordan. "We had a plan for what to do after we won them. That's what separated us from other insurgent campaigns."

This systematic approach to momentum management was particularly evident in Carter's fundraising operation. His campaign had identified potential donors in every state and maintained detailed records of their interests, capabilities, and political connections. When media coverage of his early victories demonstrated his viability, the campaign was able to quickly organize fundraising events that capitalized on his newfound celebrity status.

More importantly, Carter's momentum was reinforced by his ability to exceed expectations consistently. Because he had started the campaign as an unknown, even modest successes generated disproportionate media attention. A third-place finish became a "strong showing." A narrow victory became a "breakthrough." His campaign skillfully managed expectations to ensure that almost any reasonable performance would be interpreted as evidence of growing strength.

Carter's breakthrough might have stalled, like those of many insurgent candidates, when the primary calendar moved to larger, more diverse states where personal campaigning was less effective and organizational resources more important. But Carter possessed an asset that other breakthrough candidates lacked: a geographic base that provided both delegates and credibility for his claim to represent a new kind of Democratic politics.

The South in 1976 remained largely Democratic at the state and local level, but southern Democrats had become increasingly alienated from their party's national leadership. The civil rights revolution of the 1960s, combined with the cultural liberalism of the McGovern era, had created a gulf between southern Democratic voters and the activists who increasingly dominated the party's nominating process.

Carter's candidacy offered southern Democrats a chance to reclaim influence within their party while supporting a candidate who shared their regional identity and cultural values. As a southerner who had evolved on civil rights issues and could speak the language of both traditional and progressive Democrats, Carter was uniquely positioned to bridge these divisions.

His sweep of southern primaries in March and April 1976 provided the delegate foundation that sustained his campaign through challenges from late-entering candidates like Frank Church and Jerry Brown. More importantly, these victories demonstrated that Carter could assemble the kind of broad geographic coalition that would be necessary for general election success.

"The South wasn't just Jimmy's geographic base," noted Stuart Eizenstat, Carter's policy director. "It was proof that he could win in regions where other liberal Democrats had struggled. That made him credible to party leaders who were worried about electability."

As Carter's breakthrough became undeniable through the spring of 1976, the Democratic establishment mounted the kind of counterattack that had become predictable whenever insurgent candidates threatened to capture the nomination. Party leaders who had initially dismissed Carter as a regional candidate suddenly awakened to the possibility that their party might nominate someone they barely knew and could not control.

The "Stop Carter" movement took familiar forms: late-entering candidates like Church and Brown were encouraged to remain in the race as alternatives; labor leaders and big-city mayors withheld endorsements and hinted at convention challenges; editorial writers questioned Carter's experience and qualifications for the presidency. The attacks reached their peak before the crucial Pennsylvania primary, when several prominent Democrats publicly called for Carter to undergo more intensive scrutiny of his record and positions.

But the establishment counterattack against Carter proved less effective than similar efforts against previous insurgent candidates, for several reasons. First, Carter's breakthrough had been sustained over many months and multiple states, making it difficult to dismiss as a temporary phenomenon. Second, his victories had come in a diverse array of states—rural Iowa, independent New Hampshire, industrial Pennsylvania, southern Florida—demonstrating broad appeal rather than narrow factional support.

Most importantly, the very arguments that establishment figures used against Carter—his inexperience in Washington, his distance from traditional Democratic power centers, his independence from party orthodoxy—reinforced the outsider appeal that had driven his breakthrough in the first place. In the post-Watergate political environment, being attacked by Washington insiders was often more valuable than being endorsed by them.

"Every time someone in Washington said Jimmy wasn't qualified, it just proved his point about needing change," observed Powell. "The establishment attacks became part of our campaign message."

Carter's capture of the Democratic nomination at the July 1976 convention represented more than just the success of another insurgent candidate. It demonstrated that the post-reform primary system had fundamentally altered the requirements for presidential success, rewarding qualities—systematic organization, personal authenticity, strategic patience—that had been less important in the era of brokered conventions.

Carter's breakthrough also revealed how dramatically the Democratic Party had changed since the McGovern reforms. The coalition that nominated him included significant numbers of voters who had been alienated by the party's liberal drift in the early 1970s: southern whites, conservative Catholics, older Americans, and working-class voters who valued cultural traditionalism alongside economic populism.

This broader coalition enabled Carter to avoid the trap that had snared McGovern: being seen as the candidate of a liberal elite rather than mainstream Democratic voters. Carter's positions on many issues were actually quite liberal, but his cultural identity and personal style allowed him to present those positions in ways that seemed moderate and mainstream.

"Jimmy proved that you could be liberal on policy and conservative on culture," reflected Jordan. "That combination turned out to be exactly what Democratic voters were looking for in 1976."

Unlike most breakthrough candidates, Carter successfully translated his primary success into general election victory, defeating Gerald Ford in November 1976 by maintaining the broad coalition he had assembled during the primary season. His triumph seemed to validate the strategic insights that had driven his insurgent campaign and to prove that authentic outsiders could not only break through but also sustain their success.

Yet Carter's presidency would reveal the limitations of the very qualities that had enabled his breakthrough. The systematic approach and personal moralism that had served him well as a candidate proved less effective in governing, where success required the kind of coalition-building and political compromise that Carter had explicitly rejected during his campaign.

The authenticity that had been Carter's greatest political asset became a liability when governing required the kind of tactical flexibility and strategic ambiguity that effective presidents often employ. His independence from Washington power centers, which had been central to his appeal as a candidate, left him without the relationships and institutional knowledge necessary for presidential leadership.

"Jimmy was perfectly suited for the politics of breakthrough," one former aide reflected years later. "But breakthrough politics and governing politics require different skill sets. Jimmy never really made that transition."

Despite the mixed legacy of his presidency, Carter's 1976 breakthrough established a template for outsider candidates that would influence American politics for decades. His systematic approach to primary campaigning, his emphasis on personal authenticity, and his ability to transform political liabilities into assets would be studied and emulated by future insurgent candidates.

More importantly, Carter proved that the post-reform primary system had created genuine opportunities for candidates who understood its dynamics and were willing to commit totally to exploiting them. His breakthrough demonstrated that in American politics, there was always room for a candidate who could offer voters something genuinely different—if that candidate possessed the strategic vision and tactical discipline to navigate the complex path from obscurity to the White House.

The peanut farmer from Plains, Georgia, had accomplished something that the political establishment had considered impossible: he had captured the presidency through sheer force of will and superior understanding of how the game had changed. His breakthrough would inspire generations of outsider candidates, even as his presidency would demonstrate the enormous challenges that await those who successfully make the journey from breakthrough to governing.

“Kennedy’s campaign revealed both the potential and the limitations of breakthrough politics when applied to challenges against incumbents.”

5

KENNEDY CHALLENGE (1980)

The phone rang at Hickory Hill just after midnight on November 7, 1979, jolting Ted Kennedy from his first peaceful sleep in weeks. The voice on the other end belonged to CBS correspondent Roger Mudd, whose recent interview with Kennedy had become the talk of Washington political circles—and not in a good way.

"Senator," Mudd said without preamble, "we're getting reports that you're about to announce your candidacy for president tomorrow. Any comment?"

Kennedy sat up in bed, suddenly wide awake. For months, he had been wrestling with the most difficult political decision of his life: whether to challenge a sitting president of his own party, something that hadn't been attempted successfully since the primaries began determining nominations. The pressure from Democratic liberals had been relentless—Jimmy Carter's presidency seemed to be failing on multiple fronts, and party activists were desperate for someone who could restore the magic of Camelot to American politics.

"Roger," Kennedy said slowly, "I'll have an announcement for you tomorrow."

When Kennedy formally declared his candidacy on November 7, 1979, at Boston's Faneuil Hall, he seemed to possess every possible advantage for a breakthrough campaign. He was the heir to America's most famous political dynasty, blessed with instant name recognition that other candidates spent years trying to achieve. He was the liberal lion of the Senate, with a legislative record on health care, civil rights, and economic justice that energized the Democratic base. Most importantly, he was a

Kennedy—a name that still carried mystical power in Democratic politics, evoking memories of inspirational leadership and tragic martyrdom.

Yet Kennedy's challenge would demonstrate that even the most advantageous circumstances cannot guarantee a successful breakthrough if the candidate himself is not prepared for the brutal realities of modern presidential politics. His campaign would reveal how personal flaws, strategic miscalculations, and external events can derail even the most promising insurgency, while also showing that breakthrough moments can occur even in ultimately unsuccessful campaigns.

Kennedy's decision to challenge Carter grew from the profound disappointment that liberal Democrats felt with the president they had helped elect four years earlier. Carter had campaigned as a progressive reformer who would restore moral leadership to Washington, but his presidency had been marked by economic stagnation, energy crises, and foreign policy setbacks that seemed to vindicate Republican criticisms of Democratic governance.

More galling to liberal activists was Carter's apparent abandonment of traditional Democratic priorities. His emphasis on fiscal restraint over social spending, his deregulation initiatives, and his increasingly hawkish foreign policy positions seemed to represent a betrayal of the party's core values. By 1979, Carter's approval ratings among Democrats had fallen below 50 percent, creating an opening that Kennedy's supporters found impossible to ignore.

"Jimmy Carter had been elected as a Democrat, but he was governing like a moderate Republican," recalled Paul Kirk, Kennedy's political director. "Liberal Democrats felt homeless in their own party."

The draft-Kennedy movement that emerged in 1979 represented more than just dissatisfaction with Carter's performance—it embodied a broader belief that the Democratic Party had lost its way and needed to return to the activist liberalism of the 1960s. Kennedy supporters saw his candidacy as a chance to reclaim the party from the centrist technocrats who had dominated Democratic politics since McGovern's defeat.

This ideological foundation gave Kennedy's insurgency a passion and energy that distinguished it from typical intraparty challenges. His supporters weren't just backing an alternative candidate—they were joining a crusade to save the soul of the Democratic Party. The intensity of this commitment would prove to be both Kennedy's greatest strength and his most significant weakness.

What Kennedy's enthusiastic supporters often ignored was the enormous liability that overshadowed his candidacy: the events of July 18, 1969, when Kennedy's car plunged off a bridge on Chappaquiddick Island, killing his passenger, Mary Jo Kopechne. The incident had ended Kennedy's presidential ambitions for a decade, but many Democrats assumed that the passage of time had diminished its political impact.

They were catastrophically wrong. Roger Mudd's November 4, 1979, CBS interview with Kennedy, broadcast just three days before his formal announcement, revealed how completely unprepared the senator was to address questions about Chappaquiddick. When Mudd asked Kennedy to explain what had happened that night, the senator's response was halting, contradictory, and unconvincing—exactly the kind of performance that reinforced doubts about his character and judgment.

"The interview was a disaster," acknowledged Kennedy campaign manager Steve Smith. "We thought people were ready to move beyond Chappaquiddick, but Ted's inability to discuss it coherently showed that he wasn't ready to move beyond it himself."

The Chappaquiddick issue represented more than just a political liability—it symbolized broader questions about Kennedy's character that would plague his candidacy throughout the primary season. Voters who might have been willing to overlook personal failings in exchange for inspirational leadership found it difficult to reconcile Kennedy's liberal idealism with the moral compromises that the incident seemed to represent.

More tactically, Chappaquiddick gave Carter's campaign and Republican opponents a devastating weapon that could be deployed whenever Kennedy appeared to be gaining momentum. Unlike policy disagreements or political attacks, questions about Chappaquiddick were deeply personal and impossible to answer satisfactorily. They forced Kennedy to relitigate the most painful episode of his life while simultaneously trying to present himself as presidential material.

Kennedy's breakthrough attempt began disastrously in Iowa, where his campaign's overconfidence and poor organization combined with external events to produce a humiliating defeat that set the tone for the entire primary season. Kennedy's advisers had assumed that his name recognition and liberal appeal would be sufficient to win in a state where Democratic activists had historically supported anti-establishment candidates.

They badly underestimated both Carter's advantages as an incumbent president and the impact of international events on the campaign. The Iranian hostage crisis, which began on November 4, 1979—the same day as Kennedy's disastrous interview with Roger Mudd—had transformed Carter from a failed president into a wartime leader deserving of national unity. The Soviet invasion of Afghanistan on December 27, 1979, further reinforced Carter's position as the nation's commander-in-chief during a period of international crisis.

"We launched our campaign just as Carter was becoming politically untouchable," recalled Kirk. "Challenging a president during an international crisis looked unpatriotic, not principled."

Kennedy's Iowa campaign also suffered from organizational problems that reflected his team's inexperience with insurgent politics. Where successful breakthrough candidates had typically built grassroots organizations months before the first contests, Kennedy's campaign relied heavily on endorsements from elected officials and labor leaders—exactly the kind of establishment support that held diminishing value in the post-reform primary system.

The January 21, 1980, Iowa caucuses delivered a devastating verdict: Carter won 59 percent of the vote to Kennedy's 31 percent, a margin so large that it suggested Kennedy's candidacy was already over before it had truly begun. The defeat was made more painful by its comprehensiveness—Kennedy had lost not only among moderate Democrats who might have been expected to support Carter, but also among liberal activists who should have formed his natural base.

Kennedy's breakthrough moment came not through primary victories but through a single speech that reminded Democrats why they had been excited about his candidacy in the first place. On January 28, 1980, at Georgetown University, Kennedy delivered what many observers considered the finest speech of his political career—a soaring defense of liberal values that articulated the Democratic Party's historic mission with passionate eloquence.

"The commitment I seek is not to outworn views but to old values that will never wear out," Kennedy declared. "Programs may sometimes become obsolete, but the ideal of fairness always endures. Circumstances may change, but the work of compassion must continue."

The Georgetown speech accomplished what months of campaigning had failed to achieve: it demonstrated that Kennedy could be more than just a nostalgic reminder of past Democratic glories. For twenty minutes, he embodied the inspirational leadership that his supporters had hoped for, presenting a vision of activist government and moral purpose that contrasted sharply with Carter's technocratic approach to governance.

The speech generated exactly the kind of national media attention that breakthrough campaigns require. Editorial writers praised Kennedy's eloquence and substantive vision. Television commentators noted the marked contrast between the hesitant, defensive candidate who had stumbled through early interviews and the confident, passionate speaker who had commanded the Georgetown audience.

More importantly, the speech energized Kennedy's core supporters and attracted new ones who had been waiting to see evidence that his campaign represented more than just personal ambition or family legacy. Fundraising, which had been anemic following the Iowa defeat, suddenly picked up. Volunteers who had been demoralized by early setbacks began working with renewed enthusiasm.

"Georgetown reminded people why they had wanted Ted to run in the first place," reflected Richard Burke, a Kennedy aide. "It showed that he could still inspire people, even if he was struggling as a candidate."

Kennedy's first actual primary victory came in Massachusetts on March 4, 1980, but the triumph was less significant than the narrow defeat he suffered in New Hampshire a week earlier. In the first-in-the-nation primary, Kennedy reduced Carter's margin to just 10 percentage points—a remarkable improvement from the 28-point deficit he had suffered in Iowa.

The New Hampshire result demonstrated that Kennedy's campaign had learned from its early mistakes and was beginning to function as a credible insurgency. His organization had improved dramatically, relying less on establishment endorsements and more on the kind of grassroots activism that successful breakthrough campaigns required. His message had been sharpened to focus on economic issues where Carter was vulnerable rather than foreign policy where the president retained advantages.

Most importantly, Kennedy himself had evolved as a candidate. The tentative, unprepared figure who had stumbled through early interviews had been replaced by a more confident politician who could articulate his positions clearly and defend his record effectively. While he never fully overcame the Chappaquiddick liability, he had at least learned to address it more directly and move the conversation to other topics.

The Massachusetts victory that followed New Hampshire provided Kennedy with the breakthrough moment his campaign desperately needed. Winning his home state with 65 percent of the vote was expected, but doing so after weeks of speculation about whether he might withdraw from the race gave the victory symbolic importance far beyond its delegate count.

"Massachusetts proved that we weren't dead," said Kennedy campaign strategist Bob Shrum. "It gave us the credibility we needed to continue the fight and forced people to take our challenge seriously."

Kennedy's real breakthrough period came during the spring of 1980, when a series of primary victories demonstrated that his challenge to Carter had evolved from a quixotic protest into a genuine threat to the president's renomination. Victories in New York, Connecticut, and Pennsylvania proved that Kennedy could win in large, diverse states where personal campaigning was less important than organizational strength and media coverage.

The New York primary on March 25 was particularly significant because it marked Kennedy's first victory in a state where he had not been heavily favored. His 59 percent showing against Carter's 41 percent demonstrated that liberal Democrats remained deeply dissatisfied with the president's performance and were willing to support a challenger despite the national security concerns raised by the Iranian hostage crisis.

Kennedy's New York victory was powered by exactly the kind of coalition that successful breakthrough campaigns require: a combination of liberal activists energized by his message, traditional Democratic constituencies attracted by his family name, and protest voters who wanted to express dissatisfaction with Carter regardless of their feelings about Kennedy personally.

The victory also showcased Kennedy's evolution as a campaigner. His speeches had become more focused and effective, emphasizing economic themes that resonated with working-class voters while maintaining the inspirational rhetoric that appealed to liberal activists. His ability to work crowds had improved dramatically, as had his performance in televised debates and interviews.

"By spring, Ted had become the candidate we had hoped he would be from the beginning," recalled Kirk. "He was finally comfortable with his message and confident in his ability to deliver it."

Kennedy's breakthrough culminated not in primary victories but in his extraordinary performance at the Democratic National Convention in New York's Madison Square Garden. Despite having lost the nomination fight to Carter, Kennedy used his convention speech to deliver what many observers considered the greatest address of his political career—a passionate defense of liberal principles that overshadowed Carter's acceptance speech and reminded Democrats of their party's historic mission.

"For all those whose cares have been our concern, the work goes on, the cause endures, the hope still lives, and the dream shall never die," Kennedy declared in the speech's emotional climax, bringing delegates to their feet in a demonstration that lasted nearly forty minutes.

The convention speech represented Kennedy's ultimate breakthrough moment—the instance when his campaign transcended electoral politics to achieve something more lasting and significant. While he had failed to win the nomination, he had succeeded in articulating an alternative vision for the Democratic Party that would influence its direction for years to come.

The speech also demonstrated Kennedy's unique capacity for inspirational leadership, even in defeat. His ability to turn a losing convention appearance into a triumphant moment showed why his supporters had been so passionate about his candidacy and why his challenge had generated such intense emotions throughout the party.

"Ted lost the nomination but won the convention," observed journalist Elizabeth Drew. "His speech reminded people why the Kennedy name still had magic in Democratic politics."

Kennedy's 1980 campaign revealed both the potential and the limitations of breakthrough politics when applied to challenges against incumbent presidents. His late-season victories and convention triumph proved that even sitting presidents could be vulnerable to intraparty challenges if they had lost the confidence of their party's base. His ability to win primaries in major states demonstrated that breakthrough moments could occur even in ultimately unsuccessful campaigns.

Yet Kennedy's challenge also illustrated why insurgent campaigns against incumbents face nearly insurmountable obstacles. Carter's advantages as president—control of the party apparatus, access to federal resources, the presumption of legitimacy that comes with holding office—proved decisive in close delegate contests. External events like the hostage crisis and the Soviet invasion of Afghanistan created a rally-around-the-flag effect that made challenges to presidential leadership appear unpatriotic.

More fundamentally, Kennedy never solved the authenticity problem that plagued his candidacy from the beginning. His liberal message was genuine and passionate, but voters consistently questioned whether his personal character matched his public positions. The contrast between his inspirational rhetoric and his personal controversies created a credibility gap that he was never able to close completely.

"Ted's problem wasn't that people disagreed with his positions," reflected one campaign aide. "It was that they weren't sure they could trust him to live up to them."

Despite its ultimate failure, Kennedy's 1980 challenge had profound consequences for both the Democratic Party and presidential politics more generally. His campaign demonstrated that liberal insurgencies remained viable even during periods of conservative ascendancy, inspiring future challenges from candidates like Jesse Jackson and Howard Dean, who would embrace similar themes of economic justice and moral leadership.

Kennedy's convention speech, in particular, established him as the keeper of the liberal flame within the Democratic Party, a role he would play for the remainder of his Senate career. His articulation of progressive principles during the 1980 campaign provided a template for liberal politicians seeking to maintain their party's commitment to activist government during the Reagan era.

The challenge also revealed the changing dynamics of intraparty presidential contests. Kennedy's ability to sustain his campaign despite early defeats and continue winning primaries through June showed that the extended primary calendar created opportunities for comeback attempts that had not existed in earlier eras.

Most importantly, Kennedy's breakthrough moments—particularly his Georgetown speech and convention address—demonstrated that political success could be measured in ways beyond electoral victory. His campaign failed to achieve its primary objective of denying Carter renomination, but it succeeded in articulating an alternative vision for Democratic politics that would influence the party for decades.

Kennedy's 1980 campaign represented one of the great "what ifs" of modern American politics. Had he been better prepared for the scrutiny that presidential campaigns inevitably bring, had external events not worked so consistently in Carter's favor, had his personal history been less complicated, his breakthrough moments might have translated into sustained success.

The tragedy of Kennedy's challenge was not that he lost—incumbent presidents rarely lose renomination fights—but that his obvious talents as an inspirational leader were never fully realized at the presidential level. His ability to articulate progressive principles, his legislative accomplishments, and his capacity for growth as a politician suggested that he might have been a transformational president if he had been able to overcome the personal and political obstacles that constrained his candidacy.

"Ted Kennedy was probably the most naturally gifted politician of his generation," observed longtime Democratic strategist Bob Beckel. "But natural gifts aren't enough in presidential politics if you can't convince people to trust you with the ultimate responsibility."

The Kennedy challenge of 1980 thus stands as both an inspiration and a cautionary tale for breakthrough candidates. It showed that even the most advantageous circumstances—name recognition, passionate supporters, inspirational message—cannot guarantee success if the candidate himself is not fully prepared for the demands of presidential politics. Yet it also demonstrated that breakthrough moments can have lasting impact even when they do not lead to electoral victory, shaping political discourse and inspiring future candidates long after the campaign has ended.

The last Kennedy's quest for the presidency had ended in failure, but his voice would continue to echo in Democratic politics for another three decades, reminding his party of its highest aspirations even as it struggled to achieve them.

“What distinguished Hart’s insurgency from previous breakthrough campaigns was its explicit focus on ideas rather than ideology.”

6

HART ATTACK (1984)

The advance team had made a crucial mistake. As Gary Hart's chartered plane descended toward Manchester, New Hampshire, on the morning of February 29, 1984, his campaign manager, Bill Shore, looked out the window and felt his stomach drop. Waiting on the tarmac below was a crowd of perhaps thirty people, huddled against the February cold and looking distinctly underwhelmed by the prospect of greeting the candidate who had just pulled off the most stunning upset in modern primary history.

"This is what victory looks like?" Shore muttered to press secretary Kathy Bushkin, who was frantically trying to reach their New Hampshire coordinator on the plane's phone.

Just twelve hours earlier, Hart had shocked the political world by defeating Walter Mondale in the New Hampshire primary by 10 percentage points, transforming himself overnight from a marginal candidate into the Democratic frontrunner. But as Hart's plane sat on the Manchester tarmac while his staff scrambled to organize a proper arrival ceremony, the moment crystallized everything that would ultimately limit his breakthrough: a campaign that excelled at creating dramatic moments but struggled with the mundane logistics that sustainable success required.

Hart's emergence as the "candidate of new ideas" would represent one of the most spectacular breakthroughs in presidential primary history—a campaign that seemed to come from nowhere to challenge the Democratic establishment's chosen nominee. Yet it would also demonstrate how quickly breakthrough moments can dissipate when they encounter the grinding realities of a sustained presidential campaign, revealing the delicate balance between inspiration and organization that determines whether shooting stars become lasting successes.

Gary Warren Hartpence—he had shortened his name to Hart in 1961, claiming it sounded more "Western"—seemed an unlikely candidate to ignite a political revolution. A lawyer and one-term senator from Colorado, Hart possessed an intellectual demeanor and somewhat aloof personality that contrasted sharply with the backslapping gregariousness typically associated with successful politicians. His colleagues in the Senate respected his intelligence and legislative craftsmanship but questioned whether he had the emotional warmth necessary for national politics.

"Gary was probably the smartest person in any room he entered," recalled Bob Beckel, who later managed Mondale's campaign against Hart. "The problem was that he often acted like he knew it."

Hart's political biography read like a résumé designed for insurgent credibility. He had managed George McGovern's 1972 presidential campaign, giving him both experience with national politics and identification with the party's anti-establishment wing. He had won his Senate seat in 1974 as part of the post-Watergate class of reformers, running on themes of generational change and government accountability. His 1980 reelection victory in increasingly Republican Colorado had demonstrated crossover appeal that suggested potential for national success.

Yet by 1983, Hart's presidential ambitions seemed quixotic. National polls showed him trailing far behind former Vice President Walter Mondale, who had assembled the most formidable pre-campaign organization in modern Democratic history. Mondale had locked up endorsements from major labor unions, civil rights organizations, and elected officials across the country, creating what political reporters dubbed the "A-Team" of Democratic politics.

Hart's decision to challenge this establishment juggernaut reflected both idealistic conviction and cold political calculation. He genuinely believed that the Democratic Party needed to move beyond the New Deal liberalism that Mondale represented, embracing what Hart called "new ideas" for a changing economy and society. But he also understood that insurgent campaigns required clear contrasts with frontrunners, and generational change provided exactly the kind of compelling narrative that could break through media clutter and voter indifference.

What distinguished Hart's insurgency from previous breakthrough campaigns was its explicit focus on ideas rather than ideology. Where other challengers had typically positioned themselves as more liberal or more conservative than the frontrunner, Hart presented himself as simply newer—a representative of a different generation with fresh approaches to persistent problems.

The "new ideas" theme was both substantively serious and strategically brilliant. Hart had spent months developing detailed policy proposals that addressed emerging issues like technology, trade, and military reform. His campaign's issue papers were longer and more sophisticated than those of his competitors, reflecting Hart's belief that voters were hungry for politicians who treated them as intelligent enough to understand complex policy arguments.

"Gary understood that people were tired of politicians who spoke in sound bites and offered simple solutions to complicated problems," explained Hart's policy director, Bill Carrick. "He was willing to engage voters at a level that other candidates found too risky."

The strategic brilliance of the "new ideas" approach was that it allowed Hart to criticize Mondale without appearing to attack him personally. Rather than questioning the former vice president's qualifications or character, Hart could position their contest as a choice between past and future, between tired old solutions and innovative new approaches. This framing made Hart appear constructive rather than destructive, visionary rather than merely ambitious.

The theme also solved Hart's fundamental challenge as an insurgent candidate: how to differentiate himself from Mondale without alienating the Democratic voters who generally approved of the party's traditional positions. By emphasizing newness rather than ideology, Hart could appeal to voters who wanted change without necessarily wanting a sharp turn to the left or right.

Hart's breakthrough began not with his New Hampshire victory but with his survival of what political scientists call the "invisible primary"—the pre-election period when candidates compete for money, endorsements, and media attention that determine who will be taken seriously once actual voting begins.

Throughout 1983, Hart struggled with the classic problem facing insurgent candidates: he needed to demonstrate viability to attract resources, but he needed resources to demonstrate viability. Mondale's early lockup of major endorsements and fundraising sources left Hart scrambling for the scraps of the Democratic establishment, competing with a half-dozen other candidates for the attention of donors and activists who were not already committed to the frontrunner.

The breakthrough came through a series of small victories that gradually established Hart's credibility. His strong performances in early candidate forums demonstrated his command of policy details and his ability to articulate the "new ideas" theme effectively. His upset victory in a Wisconsin straw poll in June 1983 provided evidence that his message resonated with Democratic activists. His successful fundraising among small-dollar donors showed that his campaign could sustain itself financially without major institutional support.

"We were building credibility one event at a time," recalled Shore. "Every time Gary outperformed expectations, it became a little easier to convince people that we were for real."

Hart's invisible primary strategy also reflected his understanding of how media coverage worked in the television age. Rather than trying to match Mondale's institutional advantages, Hart focused on creating moments that would generate disproportionate attention. His detailed policy speeches might reach only small audiences, but they established his reputation as the "ideas candidate" among the political reporters who would ultimately shape public perceptions of the race.

Hart's first major breakthrough moment came in Iowa, where his strong second-place finish on February 20, 1984, exceeded all expectations and established him as a serious alternative to Mondale. With 16.5 percent of the vote, Hart finished well behind Mondale's 49 percent but far ahead of the other candidates, including John Glenn, who had been widely touted as Mondale's principal challenger.

The Iowa result was particularly impressive because Hart had invested relatively little time and money in the state, focusing instead on New Hampshire, where he believed his message would resonate more effectively. His unexpectedly strong showing suggested that the "new ideas" theme had broader appeal than even his own campaign had recognized.

"Iowa proved that there was real hunger in the party for something different," Hart reflected years later. "Voters weren't necessarily unhappy with Democratic positions, but they wanted leaders who could present those positions in new ways."

The Iowa near-miss also generated exactly the kind of media coverage that breakthrough campaigns require. Television reporters, who had largely ignored Hart's candidacy for months, suddenly began profiling him as the "surprise" of the Iowa caucuses. Newspaper columnists wrote about his detailed policy proposals and his potential as a generational alternative to Mondale. Newsweek put him on its cover with the headline "Hart's Charge."

More importantly, the Iowa result gave Hart the credibility he needed to compete effectively in New Hampshire, where the media attention and activist enthusiasm generated by his surprise showing could be translated into actual votes. For the first time in his presidential campaign, Hart had momentum—the invisible asset that can transform long-shot candidacies into genuine threats.

Hart's February 28 victory in New Hampshire represented one of the most stunning upsets in modern primary history. Starting the campaign with less than 5 percent support in state polls, he had steadily climbed throughout February as voters became familiar with his message and impressed by his performances in candidate debates.

The breakthrough came in the campaign's final week, when Hart's town hall meetings began attracting overflow crowds and his volunteers reported unprecedented enthusiasm among voters who had attended his events. The campaign's internal polling showed Hart closing rapidly on Mondale, but even optimistic projections gave him only a narrow chance of victory.

The February 28 results exceeded Hart's most optimistic hopes: he won 37.3 percent of the vote to Mondale's 27.9 percent, a margin that represented both a decisive victory and a devastating blow to the former vice president's aura of inevitability. The victory was made more impressive by its breadth—Hart had won across demographic lines, attracting support from young and old voters, liberals and moderates, college graduates and blue-collar workers.

"New Hampshire wasn't just a victory," recalled Hart strategist Paul Tully. "It was a complete validation of everything we had been arguing about the race and the party."

The media response to Hart's victory was extraordinary, even by the standards of previous breakthrough campaigns. All three television networks led their evening newscasts with Hart's upset, and newspaper headlines across the country proclaimed the emergence of a new Democratic frontrunner. Time and Newsweek both featured Hart on their covers, and his face appeared on the front pages of hundreds of newspapers that had barely mentioned his candidacy weeks earlier.

More tangibly, Hart's New Hampshire victory triggered exactly the kind of momentum effects that breakthrough campaigns depend upon. His campaign raised more money in the three days following the primary than it had in the previous three months. Volunteers flooded his campaign offices in the upcoming primary states. Democratic politicians who had been committed to Mondale began hedging their bets, while others endorsed Hart outright.

The true test of Hart's breakthrough came on March 13, 1984—"Super Tuesday"—when nine states held primaries or caucuses simultaneously. The compressed calendar, designed to give early momentum extra importance, would determine whether Hart's New Hampshire victory represented a sustainable breakthrough or merely a temporary media phenomenon.

Hart's performance on Super Tuesday revealed both the potential and the limitations of his insurgent campaign. He won in Florida, Rhode Island, and Massachusetts—victories that demonstrated his appeal could extend beyond New Hampshire's unique political culture. But he lost decisively in Georgia and Alabama, where Mondale's superior organization and African American support proved decisive.

The mixed results illustrated the fundamental challenge facing all breakthrough candidates: translating sudden momentum into the kind of systematic campaigning required for success across multiple states simultaneously. Hart's campaign, which had been perfectly sized for retail politics in New Hampshire, found itself overwhelmed by the organizational demands of competing in nine states where personal campaigning was impossible and paid advertising was essential.

"We went from running a boutique operation in New Hampshire to trying to run a national campaign overnight," explained Shore. "We simply didn't have the infrastructure to compete effectively everywhere at once."

The Super Tuesday results also revealed the narrowness of Hart's coalition. While his "new ideas" message resonated strongly with well-educated, suburban voters who valued policy innovation, it proved less effective with the working-class Democrats and African Americans who formed the core of Mondale's support. Hart's strength among what political analysts would later call "wine track" Democrats was impressive but insufficient for sustained success.

Hart's breakthrough began to unravel during a March 11 debate in Atlanta, when Mondale borrowed a line from a popular Wendy's hamburger commercial to attack Hart's emphasis on "new ideas." Looking directly at Hart, Mondale declared: "When I hear your new ideas, I'm reminded of that ad: 'Where's the beef?'"

The line, delivered with perfect timing and obvious preparation, crystallized doubts that many Democrats had been developing about Hart's candidacy. For all his talk of new ideas, critics argued, Hart had not articulated fundamentally different positions on most major issues. His proposals were often more detailed than those of his competitors, but they did not necessarily represent the kind of dramatic departure from Democratic orthodoxy that his rhetoric seemed to promise.

"'Where's the beef?' was devastating because it captured something that people were already thinking," acknowledged Hart adviser Tom Donilon. "Gary had done a brilliant job of positioning himself as the candidate of change, but when people looked closely at his positions, they weren't that different from everyone else's."

The attack was particularly effective because it played to Hart's perceived weaknesses as a candidate. His intellectual approach to politics, which had been an asset when contrasted with traditional political rhetoric, became a liability when it was characterized as all style and no substance. His aloofness, which had seemed like principled independence, began to look like arrogance or insincerity.

More damaging was the way the "Where's the beef?" attack undermined Hart's central campaign narrative. If his "new ideas" were not genuinely new, then what was the rationale for his candidacy? If he was not offering fundamental change, why should voters abandon a candidate like Mondale, who had more experience and deeper relationships within the party?

As the primary calendar moved into April and May, Hart's breakthrough encountered the mathematical realities that ultimately determine nomination contests. Despite winning more individual primaries than Mondale, Hart was losing the delegate count due to the former vice president's superior understanding of the complex rules governing delegate allocation.

Mondale's advantages were most apparent in caucus states, where his superior organization and relationships with party activists allowed him to accumulate delegates even in states where Hart was competitive in terms of popular vote. The complex system of superdelegates—party officials and elected leaders who could support any candidate—also favored Mondale, who had spent years cultivating relationships with exactly the kinds of people who occupied these positions.

"We were winning the headlines but losing the nomination," Hart campaign manager Oliver Henkel admitted years later. "Fritz [Mondale] understood that presidential nominations are won through delegate accumulation, not media coverage."

Hart's campaign also struggled with the financial realities of sustained presidential campaigning. While his New Hampshire victory had generated impressive short-term fundraising, his donor base remained relatively narrow and his ability to raise money from traditional Democratic sources was limited by his insurgent positioning. As the campaign stretched into late spring, Hart found himself increasingly unable to compete with Mondale's superior resources.

The delegate math problem was compounded by Hart's difficulty in expanding his coalition beyond the educated, suburban voters who had powered his initial breakthrough. Despite months of effort, he never developed significant support among African American voters, who constituted a crucial part of the Democratic primary electorate. His appeal among blue-collar workers remained limited, despite policy positions that should have resonated with their economic concerns.

Hart's breakthrough was further undermined by growing questions about his personal character—issues that would eventually destroy his 1988 presidential campaign but were already emerging as problems in

1984. Reports about his name change, his claimed birth year, and his marriage generated the kind of negative coverage that breakthrough campaigns cannot afford.

More fundamentally, Hart's intellectual approach to politics and his somewhat distant personality raised doubts about whether he possessed the emotional qualities that voters expected in presidents. His strength in policy details and his command of complex issues impressed political reporters and policy experts, but many voters found him cold and calculating rather than warm and inspiring.

"Gary was incredibly knowledgeable and had great ideas," observed Democratic strategist Bob Squier, who worked with several Hart opponents. "But people weren't sure they liked him personally, and that's a fatal flaw in presidential politics."

The character question was particularly damaging because it undermined the authenticity that had been central to Hart's insurgent appeal. Voters who had been attracted to his image as a different kind of politician became skeptical when faced with evidence that he was, in some ways, a typical politician who had reinvented himself for electoral advantage.

Hart's breakthrough campaign reached its climax in California, where a June 5 victory kept his candidacy alive but also demonstrated the limitations that would ultimately prevent him from sustaining his early success. His narrow win in the nation's largest state provided him with crucial delegates and maintained his claim to represent the future of the Democratic Party.

Yet even Hart's California victory revealed the narrowness of his appeal. He won primarily among well-educated, affluent voters in suburban and coastal areas, while Mondale dominated in urban centers and among working-class Democrats. The geographic and demographic patterns that characterized the California result were repeated in other large states, suggesting that Hart's coalition, while passionate and articulate, was too limited for general election success.

"California showed both Gary's potential and his limitations," reflected Hart strategist John Emerson. "He could win, but only among certain kinds of Democrats. That wasn't enough to beat Reagan."

Despite his ultimate failure to secure the nomination, Hart's 1984 breakthrough had profound consequences for Democratic politics and presidential campaigning more generally. His emphasis on "new ideas" influenced a generation of Democratic politicians who sought to modernize the party's message while maintaining its core commitments. His success in attracting educated, suburban voters pointed toward demographic changes that would reshape American politics in subsequent decades.

Hart's campaign also demonstrated the potential for breakthrough candidates to influence party direction even when they did not win nominations. His policy innovations on issues like military reform and economic modernization were largely adopted by subsequent Democratic nominees, and his critique of traditional liberalism helped lay the groundwork for the centrist "New Democrat" movement of the 1990s.

More immediately, Hart's breakthrough established him as a major figure in Democratic politics and positioned him as a potential frontrunner for the 1988 nomination. His ability to successfully challenge the most well-organized frontrunner in modern Democratic history suggested that he had solved the mystery of insurgent politics and would be even more formidable in a subsequent campaign.

The tragedy of Hart's breakthrough was that it created expectations that his personal character could not sustain. His intellectual brilliance and strategic insights had enabled him to break through the political establishment's defenses, but they could not protect him from the personal scandals that would eventually destroy his presidential ambitions entirely.

Gary Hart had proven that breakthrough moments could still occur in an era of increasingly sophisticated political organizations and media coverage. His "new ideas" insurgency had captured the imagination of millions of Democrats and forced the party to reconsider its fundamental assumptions about politics and policy. But his ultimate inability to translate breakthrough into sustained success would serve as a cautionary tale for future insurgent candidates about the difference between exciting voters and actually winning their lasting support.

“Jackson’s breakthrough culminated at the DNC, where his speech was widely regarded as one of the greatest convention addresses in modern political history.”

7

JACKSON RAINBOW (1988)

The voice coming through the radio in the rented Buick was unmistakable—the rhythmic cadences, the soaring rhetoric, the call-and-response energy that could transform a political rally into something approaching a religious revival. But as Jesse Jackson's convoy wound through the hills of West Virginia on a humid May morning in 1988, even his closest advisers were having trouble believing what they were hearing on the car radio.

"With 81 percent of precincts reporting," the announcer was saying, "Reverend Jesse Jackson has won a decisive victory in the West Virginia Democratic primary, defeating Massachusetts Governor Michael Dukakis by a margin of 45 percent to 37 percent."

Jackson's campaign manager, Gerald Austin, reached over and turned up the volume, as if increasing the sound might make the impossible result more believable. West Virginia was 96 percent white, heavily working-class, and culturally conservative—exactly the kind of state where an African American candidate's appeal was supposed to have natural limits. Yet Jackson had not only won, but won decisively, demonstrating that his "Rainbow Coalition" message could transcend racial boundaries in ways that few politicians, including Jackson himself, had dared to imagine.

"We just proved that everything they've been saying about Jesse's ceiling is wrong," Austin told the candidate, who was riding in the lead car. "This changes everything."

Jackson's 1988 breakthrough represented something unprecedented in American politics: an African American candidate who had moved beyond symbolic candidacy to become a genuine contender for the Democratic presidential nomination. His West Virginia victory was just one of seven primary wins that spring, successes that established Jackson as the most successful African American presidential candidate in history and demonstrated the power of coalition politics when executed with strategic brilliance and moral authority.

Yet Jackson's breakthrough would also reveal the enormous challenges facing any candidate who attempts to build a presidential coalition around historically marginalized communities. His remarkable achievements in 1988 would ultimately be constrained by the same racial dynamics he was trying to transcend, showing how even the most charismatic and tactically sophisticated breakthrough campaigns can be limited by forces beyond their control.

Jesse Jackson's 1988 campaign represented the culmination of a political evolution that had begun two decades earlier in the civil rights movement. As a young aide to Martin Luther King Jr., Jackson had learned the power of moral rhetoric and grassroots organizing, but he had also witnessed the limitations that racial prejudice imposed on even the most gifted African American leaders.

Jackson's decision to seek the presidency in 1984 had been controversial within the African American community, with many established leaders arguing that the country was not ready for a Black presidential candidate and that Jackson's candidacy would harm other Democratic candidates by association. His relatively weak showing in that first campaign—winning 3.5 million votes but only about 18 percent of the total—seemed to validate such concerns.

But Jackson had learned crucial lessons from his 1984 defeat that would inform his more sophisticated 1988 strategy. He had discovered that his appeal extended beyond African American voters to include other marginalized communities—Hispanics, Native Americans, poor whites—who responded to his message of economic justice and political inclusion. He had also learned that modern presidential campaigns required more than inspiring rhetoric; they demanded professional organization, strategic messaging, and the kind of tactical discipline that could translate moral authority into political power.

"Jesse understood that 1984 was his education," recalled Austin, who had managed several successful Ohio campaigns before joining Jackson's national effort. "By 1988, he was ready to run a real presidential campaign, not just a movement."

Jackson's evolution as a candidate was evident in every aspect of his 1988 operation. Where his 1984 campaign had been chaotic and underfunded, his 1988 effort was professionally managed and adequately financed. Where his earlier message had focused primarily on civil rights and racial justice, his 1988 platform emphasized economic populism that could appeal across racial lines. Most importantly, where his 1984 candidacy had often seemed more symbolic than strategic, his 1988 campaign was explicitly designed to accumulate delegates and influence the party's direction.

The theoretical foundation of Jackson's breakthrough was his concept of the "Rainbow Coalition"—a multiracial alliance of working-class Americans, minority communities, and progressive activists who shared common economic interests despite their cultural differences. The idea was both politically sophisticated and morally compelling: if disadvantaged Americans could overcome their divisions and vote as a bloc, they could exercise decisive influence in Democratic primaries and general elections.

The Rainbow Coalition strategy required Jackson to walk a delicate line between maintaining his base among African American voters while expanding his appeal to other communities. This meant emphasizing universal themes like jobs, healthcare, and education while also addressing the specific concerns of different ethnic and racial groups. It meant speaking the language of economic populism in predominantly white areas while maintaining his credibility as a civil rights leader in Black communities.

"Jesse's genius was understanding that you could build a winning coalition around shared economic interests," explained Ron Brown, who would later become Democratic National Committee chairman partly because of relationships developed during Jackson's campaign. "But he also understood that you had to respect people's cultural identities and specific concerns."

The strategy was particularly evident in Jackson's approach to Latino voters, who had been largely ignored by previous Democratic campaigns. Jackson learned enough Spanish to communicate directly with Hispanic audiences, appointed Latinos to prominent positions in his campaign organization, and developed detailed position papers on immigration reform and bilingual education. His efforts paid dividends in states like California and Texas, where Latino voters provided crucial support for his primary victories.

Similarly, Jackson courted Native American voters by visiting reservations, meeting with tribal leaders, and incorporating indigenous concerns into his platform. His appeals to poor white voters in Appalachian regions emphasized economic themes while carefully avoiding the racial rhetoric that might alienate working-class whites who shared his economic positions but remained uncomfortable with explicit discussions of race.

Jackson's first major breakthrough of the 1988 campaign came in Michigan on March 26, where his upset victory over Michael Dukakis shocked the political establishment and demonstrated that his Rainbow Coalition strategy could produce concrete results in crucial primary states. Michigan's economic problems—plant closings, job losses, urban decay—provided ideal conditions for Jackson's populist message, but few observers expected him to actually win the state's Democratic primary.

The Michigan victory was particularly significant because it occurred in a diverse industrial state where Jackson's appeal had to extend beyond his African American base to include white working-class voters who were traditionally skeptical of his candidacy. Exit polls showed that Jackson had indeed assembled the kind of multiracial coalition that his campaign had promised, winning decisive support from Black voters while also attracting significant numbers of Latino, Arab American, and white working-class voters.

"Michigan proved that the Rainbow Coalition wasn't just a slogan," Jackson declared in his victory speech. "It was a real political force that could win elections and change the direction of the Democratic Party."

The victory generated exactly the kind of national media attention that breakthrough campaigns require. Television networks devoted extensive coverage to Jackson's upset, with reporters analyzing how he had managed to defeat a better-funded opponent in a state where racial demographics seemed to favor other candidates. Newspaper editorials across the country debated the implications of Jackson's victory for both the Democratic nomination and American racial politics more generally.

More tangibly, the Michigan victory triggered the momentum effects that Jackson's campaign needed to remain competitive with better-funded opponents. His fundraising increased dramatically in the weeks following the primary, as small-dollar donors responded to evidence that his candidacy was more than symbolic. Volunteers flooded his campaign offices in upcoming primary states, and his organization began attracting the kind of experienced political operatives who had previously avoided association with his campaign.

Jackson's breakthrough momentum faced its most serious test in New York, where the April 19 primary would determine whether his Michigan victory represented a sustainable breakthrough or merely an isolated success in unusually favorable circumstances. New York's complex political landscape—with its large African American and Latino populations, influential Jewish community, and diverse array of interest groups—provided both opportunities and dangers for Jackson's Rainbow Coalition strategy.

The New York campaign revealed both Jackson's strengths and weaknesses as a breakthrough candidate. His organizational abilities were evident in the sophisticated voter identification and turnout operation that his campaign mounted in New York's complicated political environment. His rhetorical skills were showcased in a series of debates and public appearances that demonstrated his command of complex policy issues and his ability to articulate a compelling vision for American politics.

Yet the New York campaign also exposed the limitations that racial dynamics imposed on Jackson's candidacy. His relationship with the Jewish community, always complicated, was severely damaged by his association with Louis Farrakhan and his references to New York as "Hymietown" during his 1984 campaign. Despite efforts to repair these relationships, Jackson struggled to attract significant Jewish support in a state where Jewish voters constituted a crucial part of the Democratic primary electorate.

"New York showed that Jesse could build an impressive coalition, but there were some communities where his ceiling was probably fixed," acknowledged Jackson adviser Frank Watkins. "That didn't mean he couldn't win, but it meant he had to win by overwhelming margins among his base supporters."

Jackson's second-place finish in New York—winning 37 percent of the vote to Dukakis's 51 percent—was disappointing but still impressive enough to maintain his campaign's viability. He had demonstrated significant strength in the nation's second-largest state and had prevented Dukakis from achieving the kind of decisive victory that might have effectively ended the race. More importantly, he had accumulated enough delegates to ensure his influence at the Democratic National Convention.

Jackson's true breakthrough period came during May 1988, when he won a remarkable series of primary victories that established him as a genuine threat to capture the Democratic nomination. His wins in West Virginia, South Carolina, Louisiana, Mississippi, Alabama, and the District of Columbia demonstrated that his appeal could transcend the geographic and demographic boundaries that had constrained previous African American candidates.

The West Virginia victory was particularly significant because it shattered assumptions about Jackson's limitations among white working-class voters. In a state where African Americans constituted less than 4 percent of the population, Jackson's economic populism resonated with voters who were struggling with plant closings, unemployment, and the decline of traditional industries. His message about corporate responsibility and workers' rights attracted support from voters who might have been expected to be skeptical of an African American candidate from Chicago.

"West Virginia proved that class could trump race if you had the right message and the right messenger," observed political scientist Katherine Tate. "Jesse showed that white working-class voters would support a Black candidate if they believed he would fight for their economic interests."

Jackson's southern victories were equally impressive, demonstrating his ability to mobilize African American voters while also attracting significant white support in states where racial politics remained sensitive. His Louisiana victory was particularly notable because it occurred in a state with a complex racial history and showed that his message could appeal to both urban African Americans and rural white voters who shared concerns about economic inequality.

The string of May victories generated unprecedented media coverage of Jackson's candidacy, with many reporters beginning to discuss seriously the possibility that he might actually win the Democratic nomination.

His success forced a fundamental reassessment of American electoral politics, challenging assumptions about the role of race in voting behavior and the potential for coalition-building across traditional demographic boundaries.

As Jackson's primary victories accumulated, attention turned to the delegate mathematics that would ultimately determine the Democratic nomination. Despite his impressive string of wins, Jackson faced the same challenge that had confronted other breakthrough candidates: translating momentum into the systematic delegate accumulation necessary for nomination.

Jackson's campaign demonstrated a sophisticated understanding of the complex rules governing delegate allocation, maximizing his delegate haul in states where he won while limiting his losses in states where he finished second or third. His organization proved particularly effective in caucus states, where intensive grassroots organizing could overcome resource disadvantages and where his passionate supporters were willing to invest the time necessary for success.

By June 1988, Jackson had accumulated nearly 1,200 delegates—far more than any African American candidate in history and enough to ensure significant influence at the Democratic convention. His delegate total represented about 29 percent of the total needed for nomination, making him a crucial player in convention negotiations and guaranteeing that his policy positions would receive serious consideration.

"Jesse's delegate count meant that he couldn't be ignored or marginalized," explained Democratic strategist Donna Brazile, who worked on Jackson's campaign. "He had earned the right to be treated as an equal partner in determining the party's direction."

The delegate mathematics also revealed the limitations of Jackson's breakthrough. Despite his impressive primary victories and passionate grassroots support, he had not accumulated enough delegates to challenge Dukakis seriously for the nomination. His campaign had proven that an African American candidate could be competitive in a Democratic primary, but it had not yet solved the puzzle of how to build a majority coalition in a party where white voters still constituted the overwhelming majority of primary participants.

Jackson's breakthrough culminated at the Democratic National Convention in Atlanta, where his speech on July 19, 1988, was widely regarded as one of the greatest convention addresses in modern political history. The speech combined Jackson's gifts as an orator with his strategic understanding of the moment, using his platform to articulate a vision of American politics that transcended the racial boundaries his candidacy had challenged.

"America is not like a blanket—one piece of unbroken cloth, the same color, the same texture, the same size," Jackson declared in the speech's most memorable passage. "America is more like a quilt—many patches, many pieces, many colors, many sizes, all woven and held together by a common thread."

The convention speech represented Jackson's ultimate breakthrough moment—the instance when his campaign transcended the limitations of racial politics to articulate a broader vision of American possibility. His ability to command the convention's attention and respect, despite having lost the nomination fight, demonstrated the power of moral leadership and strategic persistence.

The speech also showcased Jackson's unique position in American politics as both an outsider challenging the establishment and an insider with sufficient influence to shape the party's direction. His endorsement of Dukakis was crucial for Democratic unity, but it came with explicit expectations about platform positions and campaign strategy that reflected his leverage within the party.

"Jesse's convention speech reminded everyone why he had been such a formidable candidate," observed journalist E.J. Dionne. "He may not have won the nomination, but he had fundamentally altered the conversation about race and politics in America."

Jackson's 1988 campaign revealed both the potential and the constraints facing breakthrough candidates who attempt to build presidential coalitions around historically marginalized communities. His remarkable primary victories and delegate accumulation proved that such campaigns could achieve far more than symbolic success, but his ultimate inability to capture the nomination demonstrated the persistent power of racial dynamics in American electoral politics.

The campaign's limitations were evident in several areas. Despite Jackson's efforts to build a truly multiracial coalition, his support remained heavily concentrated among African American voters, limiting his appeal in states with small Black populations. His association with controversial figures like Louis Farrakhan and his history of inflammatory statements created ongoing problems with Jewish voters and some moderate Democrats who might otherwise have been attracted to his economic message.

More fundamentally, Jackson's campaign encountered the same challenge that confronts all breakthrough candidates: the need to balance authenticity with electability. His moral authority and passionate advocacy for progressive causes inspired devoted followers, but also raised questions among some voters about whether he possessed the pragmatic skills necessary for effective governance.

"Jesse's problem wasn't that people disagreed with his positions," reflected Austin. "It was that some people weren't sure he could actually implement them if he became president."

Despite falling short of the nomination, Jackson's 1988 breakthrough had profound consequences for American politics that persisted long after the campaign ended. His demonstration that an African American candidate could win primaries across the country and accumulate significant delegate totals paved the way for future minority candidates and challenged assumptions about the limitations imposed by racial dynamics.

Jackson's campaign also influenced the strategic thinking of subsequent Democratic nominees, who recognized the importance of coalition-building across racial and ethnic lines. His emphasis on economic populism and his ability to mobilize working-class voters of all races provided a template that would be studied and emulated by future campaigns seeking to build broad-based coalitions.

Perhaps most importantly, Jackson's breakthrough helped expand participation in the Democratic primary process, registering hundreds of thousands of new voters and encouraging political engagement among communities that had previously felt excluded from mainstream politics. His campaign demonstrated that American electoral politics could accommodate voices that challenged conventional wisdom and that breakthrough moments could occur even when they required overcoming centuries of racial prejudice.

"Jesse opened doors that had been closed for generations," reflected Brazile. "He proved that America was ready for leaders who looked different and spoke differently, even if it wasn't quite ready for them to win."

Jackson's 1988 campaign stands as one of the great "what ifs" of modern American politics. His ability to win primaries across geographic and demographic lines suggested that racial barriers in presidential politics were not as insurmountable as previously believed. His sophisticated understanding of coalition politics and delegate mathematics demonstrated that breakthrough campaigns could combine moral authority with strategic competence.

Yet Jackson's ultimate inability to translate his breakthrough into a nomination victory revealed the persistent constraints that racial dynamics imposed on American electoral politics, even as late as the 1980s. His campaign had proven that an African American candidate could be competitive in Democratic primaries, but it had not yet shown how such a candidate could build the kind of majority coalition necessary for nomination.

The tragedy of Jackson's breakthrough was not that he lost—few insurgent candidates win nominations—but that his obvious talents as a coalition-builder and moral leader were never fully realized at the presidential level. His campaign had expanded the boundaries of American political possibility, but those boundaries remained sufficiently narrow to prevent him from achieving his ultimate objective.

Jesse Jackson had proven that the Rainbow Coalition was more than a slogan—it was a viable political strategy that could produce real victories and accumulate real power. His breakthrough had demonstrated that American politics was capable of change, even if that change came more slowly and with more difficulty than his most devoted supporters had hoped. The preacher from South Carolina had not reached the promised land, but he had shown millions of Americans that it was possible to see it from where they stood.

“The scandals that had nearly destroyed Clinton’s campaign ultimately made him a stronger candidate by forcing him to develop skills he had never needed in Arkansas politics.”

8

COMEBACK KID (1992)

The campaign bus was running late, the heater was broken, and Bill Clinton's voice was nearly gone from weeks of relentless campaigning in New Hampshire's February cold. As the Arkansas governor's motorcade pulled into the Merrimack Restaurant in Manchester at 11:47 PM on February 17, 1992, most political observers assumed they were witnessing the final stop of a dying presidential campaign.

The Gennifer Flowers scandal had dominated headlines for two weeks, destroying Clinton's frontrunner status and raising questions about his character that seemed to validate every stereotype about smooth-talking Southern politicians. His poll numbers had collapsed from a commanding lead to a distant second place behind former Massachusetts Senator Paul Tsongas. Major donors were fleeing, staff morale was plummeting, and political reporters were already writing Clinton's political obituary.

"Governor," asked a local television reporter as Clinton climbed off the bus, "do you have any response to the latest allegations?"

Clinton paused, his breath visible in the frigid air, and something shifted in his demeanor. The defensive, almost panicked candidate who had struggled through weeks of scandal coverage was replaced by the confident politician who had never lost an election in Arkansas. "You know," he said, looking directly into the camera, "the people of New Hampshire know that this election isn't about the past—it's about the future. And I'm going to keep fighting for that future as long as the people will have me."

It was a small moment that few people witnessed, but it captured the essence of what would become the most remarkable comeback in modern primary history. Eighteen hours later, Clinton would finish second in New Hampshire with 25 percent of the vote—a result that by any objective measure represented a clear defeat. Yet Clinton's masterful spin of that defeat as a moral victory would transform him overnight from damaged goods into the "Comeback Kid," demonstrating how breakthrough moments in politics sometimes have less to do with actual results than with the stories candidates tell about those results.

Bill Clinton's path to the 1992 Democratic nomination had seemed almost inevitable until the moment it nearly ended before it began. The five-term Arkansas governor possessed exactly the profile that Democratic leaders believed they needed to reclaim the White House: a moderate Southerner who could appeal to the conservative Democrats who had abandoned the party during the Reagan era, combined with the policy expertise and communication skills necessary to compete against a popular incumbent president.

Clinton's advantages seemed overwhelming. He had spent years cultivating relationships with Democratic activists across the country through his work with the Democratic Leadership Council, the centrist organization that advocated moving the party toward the political center. His keynote address at the 1988 Democratic National Convention, though initially ridiculed for its length, had ultimately enhanced his national profile when he appeared on "The Tonight Show" to joke about the speech with Johnny Carson.

More importantly, Clinton possessed the kind of political skills that had made him the youngest governor in America and kept him in office through multiple election cycles. His ability to connect with voters on an emotional level, his command of policy details, and his talent for finding common ground among competing factions had made him a dominant figure in Arkansas politics and suggested he could transfer those skills to the national stage.

"Bill had everything you could want in a presidential candidate," recalled Mickey Kantor, who served as Clinton's campaign chairman. "He was smart, articulate, experienced, and he understood how to build coalitions. The only question was whether he could survive the scrutiny that comes with presidential politics."

That question was answered emphatically in January 1992, when the Star tabloid published allegations by Gennifer Flowers that she had conducted a twelve-year affair with Clinton. The story, which Clinton vehemently denied, triggered exactly the kind of character-based controversy that had destroyed other political careers and threatened to end Clinton's presidential ambitions before they had truly begun.

Clinton's response to the Flowers scandal revealed both his strategic brilliance and his willingness to take enormous political risks when conventional approaches failed. Rather than adopting the typical political strategy of declining to comment on personal matters, Clinton chose to address the allegations directly in the most high-profile venue available: CBS's "60 Minutes," immediately following the network's broadcast of Super Bowl XXVI.

The January 26, 1992, interview, conducted by Steve Kroft with Clinton and his wife, Hillary, sitting side by side on a couch, was a masterclass in crisis management that would be studied by political strategists for decades. Clinton acknowledged "problems" in his marriage without confirming specific allegations, presenting himself as a flawed human being who had learned from his mistakes rather than a perfect politician hiding embarrassing secrets.

"You know, I think most Americans who are watching this tonight, they'll know we're saying they'll have to shut up," Clinton said, looking directly into the camera. "But I think most Americans will know what we're saying, and I think they'll get it. And they'll feel that, you know, we're not perfect, but that at least we're real."

The interview strategy was risky because it required Clinton to discuss his personal life in unprecedented detail, potentially providing ammunition for future attacks. But it was also brilliant because it allowed him to frame the conversation on his own terms, presenting the scandal as evidence of his honesty and authenticity rather than his dishonesty and moral weakness.

"The '60 Minutes' interview showed Bill at his best," observed James Carville, Clinton's lead strategist. "He took a potentially campaign-ending crisis and turned it into proof that he was a different kind of politician—one who would level with the American people even about difficult personal matters."

The interview generated enormous media coverage and temporarily stabilized Clinton's campaign, but it did not eliminate the scandal's impact on his New Hampshire prospects. Polls continued to show him trailing Tsongas by significant margins, and many Democratic primary voters remained skeptical about supporting a candidate whose personal life had become a subject of national discussion.

Just as Clinton's campaign appeared to be recovering from the Flowers scandal, a new controversy emerged that threatened to inflict even more serious damage to his presidential prospects. On February 12, 1992, the Wall Street Journal published a letter Clinton had written in 1969 to Colonel Eugene Holmes, the director of the Army ROTC program at the University of Arkansas, thanking Holmes for "saving me from the draft."

The letter, written when Clinton was a graduate student at Oxford University, revealed his efforts to avoid military service during the Vietnam War and included language that seemed to demonstrate his opposition to the war and his calculation in avoiding the draft. For a candidate already struggling with questions about his character and trustworthiness, the draft letter represented a potentially fatal blow to his presidential ambitions.

"The draft letter was worse than Gennifer Flowers because it raised questions about Bill's patriotism and his honesty about his military service," recalled Paul Begala, another Clinton strategist. "Flowers was about his personal life, but the draft letter was about his fitness to be commander-in-chief."

The timing of the letter's release, just six days before the New Hampshire primary, seemed designed to maximize its political damage. Clinton's poll numbers, which had stabilized following the "60 Minutes" interview, began dropping again as voters learned about his Vietnam War record. Editorial writers questioned his credibility, and several prominent Democrats privately suggested that he should consider withdrawing from the race.

Clinton's response to the draft letter controversy demonstrated the tactical evolution that would eventually make him president. Rather than becoming defensive or trying to explain away the letter's contents, he used the controversy as an opportunity to present himself as a member of the Vietnam generation who had struggled with the moral complexities of that war, just as many Americans of his age had done.

"I was opposed to the war, and I'm not ashamed of that," Clinton said at a February 13 press conference. "But I love my country, and I would never do anything to dishonor it. The question is not what I did twenty-three years ago, but what I'll do as president to keep America strong and at peace."

With his poll numbers dropping and his campaign finances strained, Clinton faced a crucial strategic decision: should he scale back his New Hampshire effort and focus on more favorable contests later in the primary calendar, or should he commit everything to a state where victory seemed increasingly unlikely?

Clinton chose to fight, making a total commitment to New Hampshire that reflected both his competitive instincts and his understanding that his campaign needed a breakthrough moment to survive. For the final two weeks before the primary, Clinton campaigned with an intensity that impressed even veteran political observers, appearing at town halls, factory gates, and coffee shops throughout the state.

The strategy required reframing the New Hampshire contest in ways that would allow Clinton to claim victory even in defeat. His campaign began lowering expectations systematically, arguing that a strong second-place finish would demonstrate his resilience and prove that the scandals had not permanently damaged his candidacy.

"We knew we weren't going to win New Hampshire," acknowledged George Stephanopoulos, Clinton's communications director. "But we also knew that if we could finish strong and control the story coming out of the primary, we could turn a loss into a victory."

The expectations game that Clinton's campaign played in New Hampshire's final weeks was a textbook example of how skilled political operators can manipulate media coverage and voter perceptions. By consistently predicting that Clinton would finish third or fourth, his advisers created a situation where any better performance would be interpreted as evidence of his comeback potential.

Clinton's New Hampshire campaign also showcased his evolution as a retail politician. The candidate who had sometimes appeared stiff and overly programmed in his early appearances became more natural and authentic as the campaign progressed, connecting with working-class voters who appreciated his policy knowledge and his apparent empathy for their economic struggles.

When New Hampshire voters went to the polls on February 18, 1992, exit polls suggested that Clinton would indeed finish second, but with a margin that could be interpreted either as a respectable showing or a disappointing defeat. Everything would depend on how the results were presented to the media and the public in the crucial hours following the polls' closing.

Clinton's final result—25.2 percent to Tsongas's 33.2 percent—represented exactly the kind of ambiguous outcome that allows skilled politicians to shape their own narrative. By any objective measure, Clinton had lost the primary decisively, finishing more than eight percentage points behind the winner. Yet his campaign's masterful spin operation turned that defeat into the foundation for a remarkable political comeback.

The transformation began with Clinton's primary night speech, delivered to a crowd of supporters at the Merrimack Restaurant, where his campaign bus had made its late-night stop the evening before. Rather than acknowledging defeat, Clinton declared victory, proclaiming himself the "Comeback Kid" who had defied the political obituaries written by his critics.

"New Hampshire tonight has made Bill Clinton the Comeback Kid!" Clinton shouted to the cheering crowd, his voice hoarse from weeks of campaigning but his message clear and confident. The phrase, coined by campaign adviser Paul Begala, would become synonymous with Clinton's political resilience and his ability to survive seemingly fatal political setbacks.

The speech was strategically timed to air on network television newscasts, where Clinton appeared energetic and victorious while Tsongas, the actual winner, seemed subdued and defensive in his victory statement. The contrast in presentation was so stark that many viewers came away from the evening believing that Clinton had actually won the primary.

"That night showed Bill's genius for political theater," observed journalist Joe Klein, who covered the 1992 campaign extensively. "He understood that in modern politics, perception often matters more than reality, and he was brilliant at shaping those perceptions."

Clinton's "Comeback Kid" narrative proved to be one of the most successful spin operations in modern political history, transforming what should have been a campaign-ending defeat into the foundation for sustained momentum that would carry him to the Democratic nomination. The key was Clinton's team's understanding of how media coverage worked in the cable television age and their ability to provide compelling narratives that busy reporters could easily adopt.

The breakthrough came in the hours immediately following the New Hampshire primary, when Clinton's campaign flooded television studios and newspaper newsrooms with surrogates who reinforced the comeback narrative. The message was consistent and simple: Clinton had been written off as politically dead, but he had fought back to finish a strong second, proving his resilience and electability.

More importantly, Clinton's campaign was able to contrast his energetic post-primary performance with Tsongas's more subdued victory statement, creating a visual narrative that suggested Clinton was the candidate with momentum despite his numerical defeat. Television producers, always seeking compelling visuals, found Clinton's celebration more interesting than Tsongas's victory speech.

"The coverage coming out of New Hampshire was all about Bill's comeback," recalled Dee Dee Myers, Clinton's press secretary. "Paul [Tsongas] won the primary, but we won the story, and in presidential politics, the story is often more important than the actual results."

The momentum generated by Clinton's "Comeback Kid" narrative had immediate practical consequences. His fundraising, which had dried up during the scandal-ridden weeks before New Hampshire, suddenly resumed as donors who had been waiting to see if his campaign could survive decided that he remained viable. Volunteers who had been demoralized by the negative coverage began working with renewed enthusiasm.

Most importantly, the comeback narrative gave Clinton credibility with Democratic voters in upcoming primary states who had been reluctant to support a candidate they perceived as damaged goods. His strong second-place finish in New Hampshire, reframed as evidence of his resilience rather than his weakness, allowed him to compete effectively in later contests where his policy positions and political skills could be more decisive factors.

Clinton's breakthrough in New Hampshire set up his decisive victories in the southern primaries, where his regional identity and moderate positions gave him overwhelming advantages over his remaining competitors.

His wins in Georgia, South Carolina, Louisiana, Mississippi, Tennessee, and Texas effectively ended the Democratic contest and demonstrated that his New Hampshire comeback had indeed transformed him from damaged goods into the party's inevitable nominee.

The southern victories revealed the strategic brilliance of Clinton's decision to fight hard in New Hampshire despite unfavorable circumstances. By surviving the early contests with his credibility intact, he had positioned himself to dominate the primaries in states where his natural advantages could be decisive. His regional appeal, combined with strong support from African American voters who appreciated his civil rights record, created an overwhelming coalition in the South.

"New Hampshire gave Bill the credibility he needed to be competitive in the South," explained Vernon Jordan, a Clinton adviser. "But once we got to our home turf, the combination of his southern identity and his moderate positions made him unbeatable."

Clinton's southern sweep also demonstrated how breakthrough moments can create self-reinforcing cycles of success. His New Hampshire comeback had generated media coverage that improved his name recognition and fundraising, which allowed him to compete more effectively in subsequent contests, which generated more victories and media coverage. By Super Tuesday, Clinton had achieved the kind of momentum that made his nomination seem inevitable.

Clinton's 1992 breakthrough was remarkable not just for its impact on the presidential race, but for the way it transformed Clinton himself as a politician. The candidate who emerged from New Hampshire was markedly different from the one who had entered the race as the presumed frontrunner, having learned lessons about resilience, authenticity, and media management that would serve him throughout his political career.

The scandals that had nearly destroyed Clinton's campaign ultimately made him a stronger candidate by forcing him to develop skills he had never needed in Arkansas politics. His ability to connect with voters on an emotional level, which had always been one of his strengths, became even more pronounced as he learned to present himself as a flawed but authentic human being rather than a perfect politician.

"The New Hampshire experience taught Bill that voters would forgive personal mistakes if they believed you were genuine about wanting to help them," observed Hillary Clinton years later. "It made him more human and more effective as a politician."

Clinton's media skills, already considerable, were sharpened by the constant scrutiny he faced during the scandal-ridden weeks before New Hampshire. His ability to stay on message while addressing difficult questions, his talent for reframing negative stories in positive terms, and his skill at using body language and tone of voice to convey sincerity were all enhanced by the crucible of the 1992 primary campaign.

Perhaps most importantly, Clinton's New Hampshire experience taught him the importance of controlling political narratives rather than simply responding to them. His "Comeback Kid" breakthrough demonstrated that skilled politicians could shape media coverage and public perceptions through strategic messaging and disciplined execution.

Unlike many breakthrough candidates, Clinton was able to sustain his New Hampshire momentum all the way to the presidency, winning both the Democratic nomination and the general election. His success revealed the key factors that distinguish temporary breakthrough moments from sustainable political success: superior organization, disciplined messaging, strategic flexibility, and the ability to learn from setbacks.

Clinton's campaign organization, anchored by experienced professionals like James Carville, George Stephanopoulos, and Mickey Kantor, provided the infrastructure necessary to capitalize on breakthrough moments and maintain momentum across a long campaign. Their understanding of media dynamics, delegate mathematics, and voter psychology allowed them to maximize the impact of Clinton's New Hampshire comeback.

More importantly, Clinton himself demonstrated the kind of personal resilience and strategic adaptability that sustainable success requires. His ability to learn from the scandals that had nearly destroyed his campaign, to evolve as a communicator and retail politician, and to maintain his focus on policy issues despite personal distractions showed that he possessed the qualities necessary for long-term political success.

"Bill's breakthrough in New Hampshire worked because he had the organizational and personal assets to sustain it," reflected Carville. "A lot of candidates can create exciting moments, but very few can turn those moments into lasting success."

Clinton's "Comeback Kid" breakthrough established a template for political recovery that would be studied and emulated by candidates facing similar crises for decades to come. His strategy of acknowledging problems without admitting specific wrongdoing, reframing defeats as moral victories, and using personal setbacks to demonstrate authenticity became standard techniques in modern political communication.

The Clinton model showed that in the media age, skilled politicians could survive almost any scandal if they responded with sufficient speed, creativity, and strategic discipline. His willingness to address personal controversies directly, rather than hoping they would disappear, became the preferred approach for candidates facing character-based attacks.

Perhaps most importantly, Clinton's breakthrough demonstrated that modern presidential campaigns rewarded resilience and adaptability more than traditional political virtues like consistency and moral rectitude. His ability to survive and thrive despite serious personal and political setbacks suggested that American voters were more interested in candidates who could solve their problems than in those who lived perfect personal lives.

Clinton's 1992 breakthrough represented both the ultimate success story of modern primary politics and a cautionary tale about the costs of such success. His remarkable comeback from near-political death to the presidency demonstrated that skilled politicians could overcome almost any obstacle through superior strategy and tactical execution.

Yet Clinton's breakthrough also revealed how the modern primary system rewarded candidates who were willing to expose their personal lives to unprecedented scrutiny and who possessed the psychological resilience to withstand sustained character attacks. The qualities that made Clinton successful—his ability to compartmentalize personal and political challenges, his talent for spinning negative stories into positive narratives, his willingness to do whatever was necessary to win—would continue to define his presidency and ultimately contribute to his impeachment.

"Bill's New Hampshire breakthrough showed both his greatest strengths and his most dangerous weaknesses," observed one longtime Clinton adviser. "He could survive anything and turn any crisis into an opportunity, but that same quality sometimes led him to take risks that other politicians would have avoided."

The "Comeback Kid" had proven that breakthrough moments could indeed be sustained and transformed into lasting political success. But he had also shown that such success came with costs that extended far beyond the campaign trail, shaping not just electoral outcomes but the very nature of American political culture for generations to come.

"Buchanan's emphasis on economic nationalism, immigration restriction, and skepticism toward global capitalism provided a template for future Republican populists."

9

BUCHANAN BRIGADES (1996)

The crowd at the American Legion hall in Littleton, New Hampshire, was unlike anything veteran political reporters had seen at a Republican primary event. Instead of the usual collection of party activists, business leaders, and suburban professionals who typically populated GOP campaign stops, the audience facing Pat Buchanan on the snowy evening of February 19, 1996, consisted largely of working-class men in flannel shirts, women worried about factory closings, and retirees angry about what they saw as their party's abandonment of ordinary Americans.

"The peasants are coming with pitchforks!" Buchanan declared to thunderous applause, his voice rising above the cheers of supporters who had never felt represented by the country club Republicans who typically dominated party politics. "We're going to take this party back from the corporate lobbyists and Wall Street money men who have forgotten what the Republican Party is supposed to stand for!"

It was vintage Buchanan—populist rhetoric delivered with the fervor of a television evangelist and the precision of the skilled communicator he had been throughout his career as a journalist and political commentator. But as the audience leaped to its feet in sustained applause, something unprecedented was happening in American politics: a conservative intellectual was leading a working-class revolt against the Republican establishment, demonstrating that populist insurgencies could emerge from either end of the political spectrum.

Less than twenty-four hours later, Buchanan would shock the political world by winning the New Hampshire Republican primary with 27 percent of the vote, defeating a field that included Bob Dole, the Senate Majority Leader and presumed nominee, along with several governors and senators who possessed far more conventional political credentials.

His victory would represent the most successful populist breakthrough in modern Republican primary history and would foreshadow political realignments that wouldn't be fully realized for another two decades.

Patrick Joseph Buchanan hardly fit the profile of a grassroots insurgent. The son of a prosperous Washington, D.C., accountant, Buchanan had graduated from Georgetown University and Columbia Journalism School before embarking on a career that had taken him to the highest levels of American political and media establishments. He had served as a senior adviser to three Republican presidents—Nixon, Ford, and Reagan—and had spent the late 1980s and early 1990s as one of television's most recognizable conservative commentators.

Yet by 1995, Buchanan had become increasingly alienated from the Republican Party he had helped build. The end of the Cold War had eliminated the foreign policy consensus that had united different factions of the conservative movement, while the party's embrace of free trade and global capitalism seemed to conflict with the nationalism and cultural traditionalism that Buchanan considered central to conservative philosophy.

"Pat had always been more of a nationalist than a pure conservative," observed his longtime friend and adviser, Bay Buchanan, who would serve as his campaign manager. "He believed in America first, and when he saw the party moving toward globalism and corporate capitalism, he felt like they were betraying working-class Americans who had supported Republicans for cultural reasons."

Buchanan's evolution from establishment figure to populist insurgent reflected broader tensions within the Republican coalition that had been building throughout the 1980s and early 1990s. The party's success in attracting white working-class voters through appeals to cultural conservatism and patriotism had created a constituency that was not necessarily committed to the economic conservatism that dominated Republican policy-making.

This tension became particularly acute as American manufacturing jobs began disappearing due to trade agreements and technological changes that Republican leaders generally supported. Working-class Republicans who had voted for the party because of its positions on abortion, gun rights, and national defense increasingly found themselves economically harmed by policies advocated by the same party they had supported for cultural reasons.

Buchanan's genius was recognizing that this tension created an opportunity for a different kind of Republican message—one that combined cultural conservatism with economic nationalism and skepticism toward the global capitalism that party elites enthusiastically endorsed. His insurgency would test whether the Republican Party was broad enough to accommodate both its country club and working-class constituencies.

What distinguished Buchanan's 1996 campaign from previous Republican insurgencies was its explicit appeal to economic anxiety and cultural resentment that crossed traditional ideological boundaries. While maintaining his conservative credentials on social issues, Buchanan adopted positions on trade, immigration, and corporate power that would have been at home in Democratic populist campaigns.

"The Republican Party has become the party of the Fortune 500," Buchanan declared in his announcement speech, "while the American worker has been forgotten." His platform called for withdrawing from NAFTA, imposing tariffs on imports from countries with cheap labor, and restricting immigration to protect American workers—positions that horrified Republican business leaders but resonated with blue-collar voters who felt abandoned by both parties.

Buchanan's "America First" message was particularly effective because it provided a coherent explanation for the economic anxieties that many working-class Americans were experiencing. Rather than accepting the conventional wisdom that globalization was inevitable and beneficial, Buchanan argued that American workers were being betrayed by political and corporate elites who prioritized profits over patriotism.

"Pat was telling people that their problems weren't their fault," recalled Greg Mueller, Buchanan's communications director. "He was saying that American workers weren't failing—they were being failed by leaders who cared more about cheap labor overseas than good jobs at home."

The message resonated particularly strongly in New Hampshire, where textile mills and shoe factories had been closing as manufacturers moved production to countries with lower wages. Buchanan's rallies in former mill towns attracted audiences that had never been part of Republican politics, including registered Democrats who were drawn to his nationalist message and criticism of free trade agreements.

Buchanan's appeal to economic nationalism was reinforced by his critique of immigration, which he argued was depressing wages and changing American culture in ways that harmed working-class communities. His opposition to multiculturalism and his defense of traditional American values provided cultural content that made his economic message acceptable to conservative voters who might otherwise have been skeptical of populist rhetoric.

Buchanan's breakthrough was powered not just by his message but by his superior understanding of how modern media worked and his ability to generate the kind of compelling content that television producers craved. His decades of experience as a television commentator had taught him how to distill complex political arguments into memorable sound bites and how to create the visual drama that cable news networks needed to fill their programming hours.

"Pat was made for television," observed CNN's Jeff Greenfield, who had worked with Buchanan on the network's "Crossfire" program. "He understood that you had to be provocative to get attention, and he was willing to say things that other politicians wouldn't say."

Buchanan's media strategy was built around generating controversy that would force coverage of his campaign and his message. His inflammatory rhetoric about immigration, trade, and cultural issues was carefully calculated to provoke reactions from his opponents and editorial writers, creating the kind of political conflict that television news thrived on.

The strategy was particularly effective in the fragmented media environment of the mid-1990s, when cable television was expanding rapidly and talk radio was becoming an increasingly important source of political information for conservative voters. Buchanan's background in both mediums gave him natural constituencies that other Republican candidates struggled to reach.

Buchanan also understood that insurgent campaigns needed different media strategies than establishment candidacies. While candidates like Bob Dole focused on traditional campaign activities like fundraising dinners and endorsement meetings, Buchanan concentrated on generating free media coverage through provocative statements and dramatic campaign events.

"We couldn't compete with Dole on money or organization," acknowledged Bay Buchanan. "But we could compete on message and media attention, and that's where Pat had natural advantages that the other candidates couldn't match."

Buchanan's breakthrough began in Iowa, where his surprising second-place finish on February 12, 1996, established him as a serious threat to the Republican establishment and set up his victory in New Hampshire eight days later. Iowa's caucus system, which rewarded intensive organization and passionate supporters, played to Buchanan's strengths as a candidate who could inspire devoted followers.

The Iowa campaign revealed Buchanan's ability to build grassroots organizations in states where his populist message resonated with economically anxious voters. His campaign attracted volunteers who had never been involved in Republican politics, including union members drawn to his opposition to free trade and working-class conservatives who appreciated his criticism of corporate power.

"Iowa showed that Pat's message had real appeal beyond the media and political establishments," recalled campaign manager Bay Buchanan. "We were attracting people who had been written off by the Republican Party but who were hungry for someone to speak for their interests."

Buchanan's 23 percent showing in Iowa, behind only Bob Dole's 26 percent, exceeded all expectations and generated exactly the kind of momentum that breakthrough campaigns require. His strong performance forced the media to take his campaign seriously and attracted the attention of conservative activists who had been looking for an alternative to the party's establishment candidates.

More importantly, the Iowa result demonstrated that Buchanan's appeal extended beyond his media celebrity to include actual voters who were willing to participate in the political process on his behalf. The campaign's ability to mobilize supporters for the intensive commitment that the Iowa caucuses required showed that his insurgency had genuine grassroots strength.

Buchanan's February 20 victory in New Hampshire represented one of the most stunning upsets in Republican primary history, demonstrating that populist insurgencies could succeed even within parties traditionally dominated by business interests and social elites. His 27 percent victory over Dole's 25 percent was narrow in terms of vote margin but enormous in terms of political impact.

The New Hampshire campaign showcased all of Buchanan's strengths as an insurgent candidate. His populist message resonated strongly with working-class Republicans who felt that their party had become too focused on corporate interests and too willing to sacrifice American jobs for global profits. His media skills allowed him to dominate television coverage and generate the kind of free publicity that his underfunded campaign could never have afforded through paid advertising.

"New Hampshire was perfect for Pat because it rewarded retail politics and authentic messaging," observed Republican strategist Mike Murphy, who worked for other candidates in 1996. "Pat could go into a factory or a VFW hall and connect with working-class voters in ways that the other candidates couldn't match."

Buchanan's victory was particularly impressive because it occurred despite overwhelming opposition from the Republican establishment. Party leaders, editorial writers, and major donors had united in opposition to his candidacy, arguing that his positions on trade and immigration would make the party unelectable in a general election.

The establishment's attacks on Buchanan often backfired by reinforcing his central campaign theme that ordinary Republicans were being ignored by party elites who cared more about respectability than results. When prominent Republicans criticized his populist rhetoric, Buchanan used their opposition as evidence that he was the only candidate willing to challenge the status quo.

Buchanan's New Hampshire victory triggered exactly the kind of political earthquake that breakthrough campaigns can create when they tap into deep voter dissatisfactions that the political establishment has ignored. His success forced a fundamental reassessment of Republican politics and demonstrated that the party's working-class base was not as committed to free-market orthodoxy as its leaders had assumed.

The immediate impact of Buchanan's breakthrough was visible in the panic it generated among Republican leaders, who suddenly realized that their party's presidential nomination might be captured by someone who opposed many of their core economic positions. Editorial writers denounced Buchanan as a dangerous extremist, while party officials began organizing efforts to prevent his candidacy from gaining additional momentum.

"The Republican establishment went into full crisis mode after New Hampshire," recalled Mueller. "They realized that Pat's message was resonating with a significant portion of their base, and they didn't know how to respond without alienating the working-class voters they needed for general election success."

Buchanan's breakthrough also forced his Republican opponents to address the economic anxieties that his campaign had highlighted. Candidates who had previously focused primarily on social issues and foreign policy suddenly began discussing trade policy and wage stagnation, acknowledging that the concerns Buchanan was raising had genuine political potency.

The media coverage of Buchanan's victory emphasized the unprecedented nature of his populist appeal within Republican politics. Television reporters struggled to categorize a candidate who combined conservative positions on social issues with liberal-sounding critiques of corporate power and global capitalism.

Despite his dramatic breakthrough in New Hampshire, Buchanan faced the same challenge that confronted all insurgent candidates: translating initial success into the kind of sustained campaign that could actually capture the nomination. His populist message, while powerful in specific contexts, proved difficult to maintain across the diverse Republican primary electorate.

The fundamental problem was that Buchanan's coalition, while passionate and committed, was too narrow to constitute a majority within the Republican Party. His appeal was concentrated among working-class conservatives who were economically anxious and culturally traditional, but he struggled to attract the suburban professionals and business-oriented Republicans who formed crucial parts of the party's primary electorate.

"Pat's ceiling was probably around 35 percent of Republican primary voters," acknowledged Bay Buchanan years later. "That was enough to win in a crowded field, but not enough to actually secure the nomination once the field narrowed and other candidates consolidated the anti-Buchanan vote."

Buchanan's campaign also struggled with the organizational challenges that confronted all breakthrough candidacies. His victory in New Hampshire had been achieved through intensive personal campaigning and superior media strategy, but sustaining that success across multiple states simultaneously required the kind of professional infrastructure that his campaign had never developed.

More problematically, Buchanan's inflammatory rhetoric, while effective at generating media attention and energizing his base, created ongoing problems with moderate Republicans and general election voters. His comments about immigration and multiculturalism were often interpreted as appeals to racial resentment, limiting his ability to expand his coalition beyond his core supporters.

Buchanan's breakthrough momentum began to dissipate in the March primaries, where his organizational weaknesses and narrow coalition became apparent. His third-place finish in South Carolina on March 2, followed by poor showings in several Super Tuesday states, demonstrated that his New Hampshire victory had been more a reflection of that state's unique political culture than evidence of broad Republican support.

The South Carolina primary was particularly damaging because it occurred in a state where Buchanan's cultural conservatism should have been an asset. His failure to compete effectively there suggested that even socially conservative Republicans were unwilling to support a candidate whose economic positions conflicted with traditional Republican orthodoxy.

"South Carolina showed that Pat's message had geographic and demographic limitations," reflected Mueller. "He could win in places like New Hampshire, where economic anxiety was high and Republican voters were more independent-minded, but he struggled in states where party loyalty and traditional conservatism were stronger."

Buchanan's campaign also suffered from the consolidation of establishment opposition that typically occurs when insurgent candidates threaten to capture major party nominations. Bob Dole's campaign, initially reeling from the New Hampshire defeat, regrouped and began running advertising that portrayed Buchanan as outside the Republican mainstream on crucial issues.

The attacks were effective because they forced Buchanan to defend positions that were genuinely unpopular with many Republican voters. His opposition to free trade, while appealing to economically anxious workers, conflicted with the pro-business orientation that most Republicans had embraced since the Reagan era.

Despite his ultimate failure to secure the nomination, Buchanan's breakthrough culminated in a prime-time speaking slot at the Republican National Convention in San Diego, where his August 12, 1996, speech became one of the most controversial and memorable convention addresses in modern political history.

The speech, which Buchanan titled "Cultural War," articulated the populist nationalism that had powered his campaign while also revealing the limitations that had prevented his breakthrough from achieving sustained success. His passionate defense of traditional values and his critique of liberal cultural influence energized conservative delegates but reinforced concerns about his appeal to moderate voters.

"There is a religious war going on in this country," Buchanan declared to a nationally televised audience. "It is a cultural war, as critical to the kind of nation we shall be as the Cold War itself, for this war is for the soul of America."

The convention speech represented Buchanan's ultimate breakthrough moment—the instance when his campaign transcended the confines of primary politics to influence the broader national conversation about conservative politics and American values. His ability to command such a prominent platform despite losing the nomination demonstrated the impact that his insurgency had achieved.

Yet the speech also illustrated why Buchanan's breakthrough had not been sustainable. His rhetoric, while inspiring to his core supporters, seemed extreme and divisive to many Americans who might otherwise have been attracted to his economic populism. The tone and content of the address reinforced perceptions that he was too polarizing to be a successful general election candidate.

Despite his failure to secure the Republican nomination, Buchanan's 1996 breakthrough had profound consequences for American politics that extended far beyond that election cycle. His demonstration that populist nationalism could attract significant support within the Republican Party presaged political developments that wouldn't be fully realized until Donald Trump's successful 2016 campaign.

Buchanan's emphasis on economic nationalism, immigration restriction, and skepticism toward global capitalism provided a template for future Republican populists who would eventually capture the party's nomination. His critique of free trade agreements and his appeal to working-class cultural anxieties identified issues and constituencies that would become central to Republican politics in subsequent decades.

"Pat was twenty years ahead of his time," observed Republican strategist Steve Bannon, who would later work for Trump. "He understood that there was a working-class constituency within the Republican Party that was being ignored by the leadership, and he showed how to appeal to those voters through nationalist rather than purely conservative messaging."

Buchanan's breakthrough also demonstrated the potential for media-savvy insurgents to disrupt established political hierarchies, even when they lacked traditional political resources. His ability to generate disproportionate attention through provocative messaging would be studied and emulated by future candidates who understood that controversy could be converted into political capital.

Perhaps most importantly, Buchanan's campaign revealed tensions within the Republican coalition that party leaders had preferred to ignore. His success in appealing to working-class Republicans on economic issues while maintaining conservative positions on social issues suggested that the party's free-market orthodoxy was not as popular among its base as its leaders had assumed.

Buchanan's 1996 breakthrough stands as one of the most prophetic failed campaigns in American political history. His populist nationalism, his critique of globalization, and his appeal to working-class cultural anxieties would all become central themes in Republican politics two decades later, when Donald Trump would successfully implement a similar strategy to capture both the party's nomination and the presidency.

The tragedy of Buchanan's insurgency was not that he lost—few breakthrough candidates win nominations—but that his obvious insights into the changing nature of American politics were dismissed by party leaders who preferred to maintain ideological consistency rather than adapt to their changing electoral coalition.

Buchanan had identified the fault lines that would eventually reshape American politics: the tension between globalization and nationalism, the conflict between corporate interests and working-class needs, and the challenge of maintaining cultural solidarity in an increasingly diverse society. His breakthrough had demonstrated that these issues could mobilize significant political support, but the Republican Party in 1996 was not yet ready to embrace the implications of his message.

"Pat saw the future of Republican politics before anyone else did," reflected Bay Buchanan years later. "He understood that the party's working-class supporters cared more about jobs and borders than they did about tax cuts and trade deals. It just took twenty years for the rest of the party to catch up."

The pitchfork rebellion that Buchanan had led in 1996 would eventually succeed, but under different leadership and in a political environment that had been transformed by the very trends that Buchanan had identified. His breakthrough had been premature but not wrong, prophetic but not sustainable, a shooting star that had illuminated a political landscape that most observers were not yet ready to see.

"Despite his defeat, McCain demonstrated that independent voters could be mobilized through influenced campaign strategies for years to come."

10

MCCAIN SURGE (2000)

The Straight Talk Express was running behind schedule, as usual. The converted campaign bus carrying John McCain through the snowy back roads of New Hampshire on February 1, 2000, had been delayed by yet another impromptu stop—this time at a diner in Peterborough where the Arizona senator had spent forty-five minutes answering questions from voters who seemed genuinely surprised to encounter a presidential candidate willing to discuss any topic they raised.

"Senator," called out Mike Murphy, McCain's media strategist, from the front of the bus, "we're going to be late for the town hall in Keene."

McCain looked up from the notebook where he had been scrawling answers to written questions submitted by passengers—including several reporters who had initially boarded the bus as skeptical observers but had gradually become something approaching believers in his unconventional approach to presidential campaigning.

"Let me ask you something, Murph," McCain replied, his voice carrying the slight rasp that came from decades of smoking and years of answering hostile questions from Vietnamese interrogators. "Would you rather we show up on time for a scripted event, or would you rather we actually talk to voters about the things they care about?"

It was a quintessentially McCain moment—the kind of authentic, unscripted exchange that had made his campaign bus the most sought-after assignment in political journalism and had transformed a long-shot candidacy into the most compelling story of the 2000 presidential race. But it also captured the essential contradiction that would ultimately limit McCain's breakthrough: his greatest strength as a candidate—his willingness to speak honestly about difficult subjects—would prove to be a strategic weakness in a political system that rewarded message discipline and tactical calculation.

Seven days later, McCain would shock the political establishment by defeating George W. Bush in the New Hampshire Republican primary by 18 percentage points, the largest margin of victory in a contested New Hampshire primary in modern political history. His breakthrough would demonstrate that authenticity and media savvy could still triumph over superior organization and financial resources, but it would also reveal how quickly such advantages could be neutralized when they encountered the full force of an aroused political establishment.

John McCain's path to presidential politics had been unlike that of any other major candidate in modern American history. The son and grandson of Navy admirals, McCain had followed family tradition into military service, but his career had been defined more by courage and controversy than by conventional success. His five and a half years as a prisoner of war in Vietnam had given him a moral authority that few politicians could match, but his reputation as a maverick within the Republican Party had also made him suspect among conservative activists who valued loyalty above independence.

McCain's Senate career had been marked by exactly the kind of bipartisan coalition-building and principled independence that made for good governance but problematic presidential politics. His work on campaign finance reform with Democrat Russ Feingold had earned him enemies among Republican donors, while his criticism of the religious right had alienated evangelical voters who formed a crucial part of the GOP base.

"John was always more interested in doing what he thought was right than in doing what was politically smart," observed his longtime adviser John Weaver. "That made him an effective senator, but it also meant he started the presidential race with a lot of built-in opposition within his own party."

McCain's decision to seek the presidency in 2000 reflected both his ambition and his frustration with what he saw as the small-mindedness of contemporary politics. At 63, he understood that this would likely be his only realistic chance for the White House, but he also believed that his experience and independence could offer voters something different from the scripted, focus-group-tested candidates who typically sought the presidency.

The challenge was how to convert his maverick reputation into the kind of broad political appeal that could overcome the enormous advantages possessed by George W. Bush, the Texas governor who had assembled the most formidable pre-campaign organization in Republican history. Bush's combination of name recognition, fundraising prowess, and establishment support seemed to make his nomination inevitable, leaving McCain and the other Republican candidates to compete for the role of principled also-ran.

McCain's breakthrough began with a strategic insight that would revolutionize presidential campaigning: in the modern media environment, authenticity and accessibility could be converted into political capital that might substitute for traditional campaign resources. The "Straight Talk Express"—McCain's campaign bus that provided unprecedented access to the candidate for reporters and voters alike—was more than just a transportation vehicle; it was a rolling advertisement for a different kind of politics.

The bus strategy was born partly from necessity and partly from McCain's understanding of how political journalism worked in the cable television age. His campaign lacked the financial resources to compete with Bush on paid advertising, but it could generate enormous amounts of free media coverage by providing reporters with the kind of compelling content that their editors and producers desperately needed.

"The bus was brilliant because it solved two problems at once," explained Murphy. "It gave us a way to reach voters without spending money on advertising, and it gave reporters a story that was different from the usual campaign coverage they were tired of writing."

McCain's approach to media relations was revolutionary in its transparency. Where other campaigns carefully controlled access to their candidates and scripted every public appearance, McCain made himself available to reporters for hours at a time, answering any question they asked with a candor that was both refreshing and occasionally politically damaging.

The strategy extended beyond media relations to encompass McCain's entire approach to voter contact. His town hall meetings were genuinely interactive, with McCain encouraging tough questions and providing detailed, unrehearsed answers that demonstrated both his knowledge and his willingness to acknowledge uncertainty or complexity. Voters who attended McCain events often left with the sense that they had encountered a real person rather than a political performer.

"John understood that people were hungry for authenticity in their political leaders," observed McCain's New Hampshire coordinator, Mike Dennehy. "He was willing to be vulnerable and honest in ways that other politicians weren't, and that created a connection with voters that transcended normal political categories."

McCain's breakthrough required a state where his unconventional approach could be most effective, and New Hampshire provided exactly the right environment for his insurgent campaign. The state's tradition of retail politics, its independent-minded electorate, and its early position in the primary calendar created ideal conditions for a candidate who excelled at personal campaigning and media generation.

New Hampshire's political culture particularly favored McCain's style of campaigning. The state's voters expected to meet presidential candidates personally and to evaluate them based on direct interaction rather than television advertising. McCain's willingness to spend hours answering questions in small venues, his comfort with confrontational exchanges, and his obvious enjoyment of political combat all played to New Hampshire's preferences.

The state's large population of independent voters, who could participate in either party's primary, also provided McCain with a natural constituency. These voters, many of whom were skeptical of both parties' orthodoxies, were attracted to McCain's reputation for independence and his criticism of partisan politics. His positions on issues like campaign finance reform and environmental protection appealed to independents who might not have been comfortable supporting more conventional Republican candidates.

"New Hampshire was perfect for John because it rewarded exactly the qualities that made him different," reflected Dennehy. "His authenticity, his willingness to take tough questions, his independence from party orthodoxy—all of that played better in New Hampshire than it would have in most other states."

McCain's New Hampshire strategy also capitalized on the changing media landscape of 2000. The proliferation of cable television news programs created an enormous appetite for political content, and McCain's bus provided a steady stream of compelling footage and quotable moments. His campaign understood that in the new media environment, creating interesting content was often more valuable than buying expensive advertising.

One of McCain's most strategically significant decisions was his choice to skip the Iowa caucuses entirely, concentrating his limited resources on New Hampshire while allowing Bush and other candidates to compete in Iowa without opposition. The decision was controversial within his campaign and was widely criticized by political experts who argued that no Republican could win the nomination without competing seriously in Iowa.

"A lot of people thought we were crazy to skip Iowa," acknowledged Weaver. "But we understood that our resources were limited and that John's message would play better in New Hampshire than in Iowa. We decided to bet everything on one state rather than spreading ourselves thin across multiple contests."

The Iowa bypass strategy reflected McCain's understanding that breakthrough campaigns often require dramatic gestures that distinguish them from conventional approaches. By publicly announcing that he would not compete in Iowa, McCain created a narrative that emphasized his independence from traditional political calculations and his willingness to take risks that other candidates wouldn't consider.

The strategy also allowed McCain to present his New Hampshire campaign as a do-or-die effort that would determine whether his insurgency could succeed. This narrative created additional media interest and gave his New Hampshire supporters a sense of participating in a historic effort to change American politics.

More practically, the Iowa bypass allowed McCain to spend the crucial final weeks before New Hampshire campaigning exclusively in that state while his opponents were dividing their time between Iowa and New Hampshire. This concentration of effort proved decisive in building the organizational strength and voter relationships that powered his eventual breakthrough.

McCain's relationship with the media became the defining characteristic of his campaign and the primary driver of his breakthrough. His openness with reporters, his willingness to discuss any subject, and his obvious enjoyment of the give-and-take of political journalism created a dynamic that was unprecedented in modern presidential politics.

The Straight Talk Express became a rolling seminar on American politics, with McCain providing reporters not just with quotes and photo opportunities but with genuine insights into the political process and his own thinking about major issues. Journalists who had grown accustomed to carefully managed campaigns found McCain's accessibility and candor irresistible.

"Covering McCain was like covering a completely different kind of politician," observed CNN's Candy Crowley, who spent considerable time on the bus. "He would answer any question, even if the answer hurt him politically. That was so unusual that it became a story in itself."

The media coverage that McCain generated created a feedback loop that amplified his political impact far beyond what his campaign resources would normally have supported. Television networks featured stories about his bus and his unconventional approach to campaigning. Newspaper columnists wrote admiringly about his willingness to discuss difficult subjects. Magazine profiles presented him as a different kind of Republican who could appeal to independent voters.

This coverage was particularly valuable because it reached exactly the kinds of voters who were most likely to support McCain: educated independents and moderate Republicans who followed politics closely and were attracted to candidates who seemed authentic and thoughtful. The free media that McCain generated through his bus strategy was probably worth millions of dollars in paid advertising.

McCain's victory in the February 1, 2000, New Hampshire primary exceeded even his campaign's most optimistic projections. His 49 percent to 31 percent victory over Bush represented not just a numerical defeat of the frontrunner but a complete validation of his unconventional campaign strategy and his bet that authenticity could triumph over organization.

The margin of victory was particularly impressive because it occurred despite Bush's superior financial resources and organizational advantages. The Texas governor had spent far more money in New Hampshire and had secured endorsements from most of the state's Republican establishment, yet McCain's grassroots campaign and media strategy had proven more effective at actually persuading voters.

Exit polls revealed the breadth of McCain's coalition, which included not just independent voters but also significant numbers of Republicans who were attracted to his message of reform and authenticity. His appeal crossed demographic lines, attracting support from both young and elderly voters, from college graduates and high school dropouts, from urban and rural areas.

"New Hampshire proved that there was a real hunger in the electorate for something different," McCain declared in his victory speech. "The people of this state have started a prairie fire that will sweep across America and give our government back to the people who own it."

The victory generated exactly the kind of national media coverage that breakthrough campaigns require. Television networks devoted extensive coverage to McCain's upset, with reporters analyzing how he had managed to defeat a better-funded opponent who had seemed inevitable just weeks earlier. Newspaper headlines across the country proclaimed the emergence of a new Republican frontrunner and speculated about the implications of McCain's victory for the general election.

McCain's New Hampshire breakthrough triggered the classic momentum effects that can transform insurgent campaigns into genuine threats to the political establishment. His fundraising, which had been adequate but unspectacular before New Hampshire, suddenly exploded as small-dollar donors responded to his victory and his reformist message.

In the week following New Hampshire, McCain's campaign raised more money than it had in the previous three months combined. The sudden influx of cash allowed his organization to expand rapidly, hiring staff and organizing in upcoming primary states where they had previously maintained only minimal presences.

More importantly, McCain's victory forced the media to reassess the Republican race entirely. Coverage that had previously focused on Bush's inevitable nomination suddenly emphasized the possibility of a genuine contest between different visions of Republican politics. McCain's reformist message, his criticism of special interests, and his appeal to independent voters created a narrative about political change that dominated news coverage for weeks.

"New Hampshire completely changed the dynamic of the race," observed Republican strategist Scott Reed, who was working for other candidates. "Suddenly, McCain was the story, and Bush was on the defensive. That kind of momentum is incredibly valuable in presidential politics because it creates its own reality."

The momentum also attracted endorsements from unexpected sources, including some moderate Republicans who had previously remained neutral in the race. Editorial boards across the country praised McCain's victory and urged Republican voters to consider supporting his reform agenda. Several prominent moderate Republicans, including some who had previously been committed to Bush, began expressing public support for McCain's candidacy.

McCain's breakthrough faced its crucial test in South Carolina, where the February 19 primary would determine whether his New Hampshire victory represented a sustainable insurgency or merely a regional anomaly. South Carolina's Republican electorate was far more conservative than New Hampshire's, with a large evangelical population and strong military presence that should have been natural constituencies for different aspects of McCain's appeal.

The South Carolina campaign revealed both McCain's potential and his limitations as a national candidate. His military record and his hawkish positions on defense issues resonated strongly with the state's large veteran population, while his authenticity and straight-talking style attracted voters who were tired of conventional political rhetoric.

Yet McCain's campaign also encountered the organized opposition of the Republican establishment, which had been shocked by his New Hampshire victory and was determined to prevent his insurgency from gaining additional momentum. Bush's campaign, backed by the political network of his father's administration and the financial resources of major Republican donors, launched an aggressive effort to portray McCain as unstable and unreliable.

"South Carolina was where the Republican establishment decided to make its stand," reflected Weaver. "They understood that if John won there, he might actually get the nomination, and they weren't going to let that happen without a fight."

The South Carolina campaign also exposed McCain's difficulties with the Republican Party's conservative base. His criticism of evangelical leaders like Pat Robertson and Jerry Falwell, while popular with independent voters, alienated religious conservatives who formed a crucial part of the state's Republican primary electorate. His positions on campaign finance reform and other issues were viewed with suspicion by conservative activists who valued ideological purity above political reform.

The South Carolina primary became a laboratory for the kind of negative campaigning that McCain's reformist message had explicitly criticized, demonstrating how quickly political establishments could mobilize against insurgent threats. Bush's campaign, along with independent groups supporting his candidacy, launched a series of attacks that questioned McCain's stability, his positions, and even his record as a prisoner of war.

The attacks were particularly effective because they exploited McCain's greatest weakness as a candidate: his legendary temper and his tendency to respond to criticism with additional criticism rather than strategic silence. Bush's supporters successfully baited McCain into exchanges that made him appear erratic and vindictive, undermining the image of steady leadership that his campaign had been trying to project.

"The South Carolina campaign showed John at his worst," acknowledged one McCain adviser years later. "Instead of staying focused on his reform message, he got drawn into exactly the kind of negative politics that his campaign was supposed to be changing."

The negative campaigning was particularly damaging because it conflicted with the narrative that had powered McCain's breakthrough. Voters who had been attracted to his authenticity and his criticism of traditional politics found themselves witnessing exactly the kind of nasty campaign tactics that McCain had promised to eliminate.

McCain's response to the attacks also revealed his strategic limitations as a presidential candidate. Rather than rising above the fray or finding ways to turn the attacks to his advantage, he often responded with his own negative comments that made him appear as calculating and political as the opponents he was criticizing.

McCain's 53 percent to 42 percent defeat in South Carolina represented more than just a tactical setback—it demonstrated the limitations that would ultimately prevent his breakthrough from achieving sustained success. Despite running a credible campaign and attracting significant support, McCain had been unable to overcome the combined advantages of establishment opposition and conservative skepticism.

The South Carolina results revealed the narrowness of McCain's coalition, which remained heavily dependent on independent voters and moderate Republicans who formed minorities within the party's primary electorate. His appeal among conservative Republicans, while real, was insufficient to overcome the suspicions that his reform agenda and maverick reputation had created among party loyalists.

"South Carolina showed that John's ceiling within the Republican Party was probably around 45 percent," reflected Murphy. "That was enough to win in New Hampshire, where independents could vote, but it wasn't enough to win in states with closed primaries where only Republicans could participate."

McCain's defeat also demonstrated how quickly momentum could dissipate when breakthrough campaigns encountered organized opposition. The establishment counterattack that had been building since New Hampshire reached full force in South Carolina, where Bush's superior organization and resources proved decisive in close contests.

Perhaps most importantly, the South Carolina campaign revealed McCain's inability to maintain the disciplined message control that sustainable presidential campaigns require. His tendency to respond to attacks with his own attacks, his willingness to engage in exactly the kind of negative politics his campaign had criticized, undermined the authenticity that had been central to his appeal.

McCain's breakthrough officially ended on Super Tuesday, March 7, 2000, when he won only four of the thirteen Republican contests and effectively ceded the nomination to Bush. The results demonstrated that his New Hampshire victory, while impressive, had not created the kind of broad-based support necessary for sustained success in presidential primaries.

The Super Tuesday defeats were particularly crushing because they occurred in states where McCain should have been competitive. His losses in California, New York, and Ohio—states with large populations of independent and moderate voters—showed that his appeal was more limited than his breakthrough had suggested.

"Super Tuesday was brutal because it showed that New Hampshire had been more of an outlier than we had realized," acknowledged Dennehy. "John's message worked great in New Hampshire, but it didn't translate as well to other states with different political cultures."

The results also revealed the organizational limitations that had constrained McCain's campaign from the beginning. His decision to skip Iowa and concentrate on New Hampshire had created a breakthrough, but it had also left his campaign unprepared for the organizational demands of competing simultaneously in multiple states.

McCain's fundraising, while improved after New Hampshire, remained insufficient to compete effectively with Bush's superior financial resources across multiple expensive media markets. His grassroots organization, while enthusiastic, lacked the professional competence necessary for the complex logistical challenges of Super Tuesday campaigning.

On March 9, 2000, two days after Super Tuesday, McCain announced the suspension of his presidential campaign, acknowledging that Bush had effectively secured the Republican nomination. His withdrawal statement captured both the disappointment of his supporters and his understanding that his breakthrough had ultimately been insufficient to overcome the structural advantages that establishment candidates possessed.

"I entered this race because I believed America deserved better than the small-minded politics of personal destruction and partisan advantage," McCain said in his withdrawal speech. "I believed that our democracy could be renewed by candidates who spoke honestly about the challenges facing our country and who offered real solutions rather than poll-tested sound bites."

The suspension represented the end of one of the most compelling breakthrough campaigns in modern political history, but it also established McCain as a major figure in American politics whose influence would extend far beyond the 2000 election cycle. His campaign had demonstrated that authenticity and reform-minded politics could attract significant support, even if they were ultimately insufficient to overcome entrenched political advantages.

Despite his ultimate defeat, McCain's 2000 breakthrough had profound consequences for American politics that extended far beyond that election cycle. His demonstration that independent voters could be mobilized through authentic campaigning and reformist messaging influenced campaign strategies for years to come, while his criticism of special interests and partisan politics helped establish themes that would become central to American political discourse.

McCain's media strategy, particularly his use of the campaign bus to generate free coverage and build relationships with reporters, became a template that would be copied by numerous subsequent candidates. His understanding that authenticity could be converted into political capital influenced a generation of politicians who sought to emulate his direct, unscripted approach to campaigning.

Perhaps most importantly, McCain's breakthrough established him as the Republican Party's most prominent critic of traditional politics, a role that would define the remainder of his political career. His presidential campaign had failed, but it had succeeded in positioning him as the voice of Republican reform and political authenticity—credentials that would serve him well in his 2008 presidential campaign and throughout his Senate career.

"John's 2000 campaign didn't win the nomination, but it won something more important," reflected Weaver years later. "It proved that American voters were hungry for political leaders who would tell them the truth, even when that truth was uncomfortable. That lesson influenced American politics for decades."

McCain's 2000 breakthrough stands as perhaps the purest example of how authenticity and media savvy can create political momentum that transcends traditional campaign advantages. His Straight Talk Express demonstrated that in the modern media environment, compelling content and genuine accessibility could substitute for superior organization and financial resources, at least temporarily.

Yet McCain's ultimate failure also revealed the limitations that constrain authentic insurgencies in American presidential politics. His unwillingness to moderate his positions or temper his rhetoric to appeal to broader constituencies ultimately limited his coalition to a passionate but insufficient minority of Republican primary voters.

The tragedy of McCain's breakthrough was not that he lost—most insurgent campaigns fail—but that his obvious talents for leadership and his genuine commitment to political reform were never fully realized at the presidential level. His campaign had shown that American voters were indeed hungry for authenticity and reform, but it had also shown that such hunger was not sufficient to overcome the structural advantages that establishment candidates possessed.

John McCain had proven that the political system remained open to insurgent challenges and that breakthrough moments could still occur when candidates offered voters something genuinely different. His straight talk had not taken him to the White House, but it had demonstrated that in American politics, authenticity remained a powerful force—even when it was not quite powerful enough to overcome the advantages of superior organization, greater resources, and establishment support.

The maverick senator from Arizona had created one of the most memorable and inspiring campaigns in modern political history, but he had also learned the hard lesson that breakthrough and sustainability require different qualities—and that possessing one did not guarantee achieving the other.

“The media’s obsession with the Dean Scream reflected the kind of pack journalism that can destroy political candidacies in the modern media era.”

11

DEAN SCREAM (2004)

The crowd at the Val-Air Ballroom in West Des Moines was electric with anticipation as Howard Dean took the stage on the night of January 19, 2004. For months, the former Vermont governor had been the most compelling story in Democratic politics—the insurgent candidate whose passionate opposition to the Iraq War and revolutionary use of the internet had transformed him from a virtual unknown into the presumed Democratic frontrunner.

But as Dean looked out at the sea of orange-clad supporters who had gathered for what was supposed to be his Iowa victory celebration, he knew that everything had gone terribly wrong. The entrance polls his campaign had conducted throughout the day had shown him finishing a strong second, close enough to John Kerry to claim momentum heading into New Hampshire. Instead, with 95 percent of precincts reporting, Dean was stuck in third place with just 18 percent of the vote, behind both Kerry and John Edwards in a result that represented not just a tactical defeat but a complete collapse of his carefully constructed insurgency.

"We're going to South Carolina, Oklahoma, and Arizona!" Dean shouted to his disappointed supporters, his voice straining to be heard over the crowd noise that the campaign's sound engineers had failed to account for. "And North Dakota and New Mexico! We're going to California, Texas, and New York! And we're going to South Dakota, Oregon, Washington, and Michigan! And then we're going to Washington, D.C., to take back the White House! YEEEAHHH!"

The primal scream that punctuated Dean's litany of states would become one of the most infamous moments in modern political history—a fifteen-second clip that would be replayed thousands of times on television and would effectively end the presidential ambitions of a candidate who had revolutionized political campaigning. But the "Dean Scream," as it became known, was merely the dramatic conclusion to a political tragedy that had been building for months: the story of how the most innovative breakthrough campaign of the internet age had destroyed itself through strategic miscalculations and the candidate's own inability to manage the pressures of national political scrutiny.

Howard Dean's path to political prominence had been marked more by pragmatic governance than by revolutionary fervor. As governor of Vermont from 1991 to 2003, Dean had established a reputation as a fiscal conservative and social moderate who balanced budgets, expanded healthcare coverage, and signed the nation's first civil unions law—accomplishments that placed him squarely in the mainstream of New England Democratic politics.

Yet by 2003, Dean had transformed himself into the voice of the Democratic Party's anti-war wing, running for president on a platform that explicitly rejected the cautious centrism that had defined Democratic politics since Bill Clinton's presidency. His opposition to the Iraq War, his criticism of the party establishment's timid response to George W. Bush's policies, and his promise to represent "the Democratic wing of the Democratic Party" had electrified liberal activists who felt abandoned by their party's leadership.

"Howard was always more of a practical politician than an ideological firebrand," observed his longtime aide Kate O'Connor. "But the Iraq War and Bush's policies genuinely outraged him, and when he started speaking about those issues, he discovered he could connect with voters in ways he had never experienced before."

Dean's transformation from pragmatic governor to insurgent candidate reflected broader tensions within the Democratic Party following the 2002 midterm elections, when Republicans had gained seats despite a weak economy and growing concerns about the Iraq War. Many Democratic activists blamed their party's losses on its failure to provide clear alternatives to Republican policies, creating an opening for a candidate who would offer passionate opposition rather than tactical moderation.

The challenge for Dean was how to channel his newfound passion into the kind of systematic campaign that could challenge better-known opponents like John Kerry, John Edwards, and Joe Lieberman. His late entry into the race and his lack of national political experience meant that he would need to build a presidential campaign from scratch while simultaneously introducing himself to Democratic primary voters across the country.

What transformed Dean from a regional candidate into a national phenomenon was his campaign's pioneering use of the internet to build grassroots support and raise money from small donors. Working with consultants like Joe Trippi, who understood the political potential of emerging digital technologies, Dean's campaign created the first truly internet-driven presidential candidacy in American history.

The centerpiece of Dean's internet strategy was his campaign's use of Meetup.com, a website that allowed supporters to organize local meetings and events without direct supervision from the campaign headquarters. Within months, Dean had more people attending Meetup events than all of his competitors combined, creating a grassroots network that extended into every early primary state and many general election battlegrounds.

"The internet allowed us to do things that had never been possible before," recalled Trippi, Dean's campaign manager. "We could organize supporters in real time, raise money from small donors across the country, and create a sense of community among people who had never met but shared our political goals."

The internet also revolutionized Dean's fundraising, allowing his campaign to collect millions of dollars from contributors who gave twenty-five or fifty dollars at a time through the campaign's website. This approach not only provided financial resources but also created an army of invested supporters who had made personal financial commitments to Dean's success.

By the summer of 2003, Dean's internet-driven campaign had begun attracting national media attention that transformed his insurgency into a genuine threat to the Democratic establishment. Magazine profiles portrayed him as a different kind of politician who was harnessing new technologies to challenge traditional power structures. Television reports about his online fundraising and grassroots organizing suggested that he was building a political movement rather than just running a campaign.

"The internet coverage created a feedback loop that made Howard seem more successful than he actually was," acknowledged one Dean adviser years later. "The media was fascinated by our technology, and that fascination translated into the kind of coverage that made us appear to be winning even when we were still building our organization."

Dean's breakthrough was powered not just by technological innovation but by a political message that resonated with Democratic primary voters who were frustrated by their party's response to the Bush administration. His willingness to criticize the Iraq War from the beginning, his attacks on Democratic leaders who had supported the invasion, and his promise to fight rather than accommodate created a clear contrast with his more cautious competitors.

"I want to be the candidate for guys with Confederate flags in their pickup trucks," Dean said in a November 2003 interview, attempting to explain his appeal to working-class voters who had been attracted to Republican candidates for cultural reasons. The comment, while poorly phrased, reflected Dean's understanding that Democrats needed to expand their coalition beyond traditional liberal constituencies if they hoped to defeat Bush.

Dean's anti-war message was particularly effective because it provided Democratic voters with a simple explanation for their party's recent electoral failures. Rather than accepting the conventional wisdom that Democrats needed to move toward the center to win elections, Dean argued that the party's problems stemmed from its failure to offer voters clear alternatives to Republican policies.

"Howard understood that Democratic voters were angry," observed Democratic strategist Bob Shrum, who worked for other candidates in 2004. "They were angry about the war, angry about the economy, and angry about their own party's inability to stand up to Bush. Howard gave them permission to express that anger."

The message resonated particularly strongly with younger voters and college-educated professionals who had opposed the Iraq War from the beginning and who felt that their views had been ignored by Democratic leaders in Washington. Dean's rallies attracted audiences that were notably younger and more energetic than typical political events, creating the kind of visual excitement that television producers found irresistible.

By late 2003, Dean's combination of internet innovation and anti-war messaging had transformed him from an unlikely insurgent into the presumed Democratic nominee. National polls showed him leading in Iowa and New Hampshire, while his fundraising had surpassed that of all his competitors. Major Democratic figures began endorsing his candidacy, and political reporters started writing about his general election strategy rather than his primary campaign.

Yet Dean's emergence as the frontrunner created new challenges that his campaign was unprepared to handle. The scrutiny that comes with leading in presidential polls revealed aspects of his record and temperament that conflicted with his image as an inspirational progressive leader. His moderate positions as Vermont governor on issues like gun control and fiscal policy raised questions among liberal activists about his ideological authenticity.

More problematically, Dean's rise attracted the kind of coordinated opposition from his Democratic competitors that typically confronts breakthrough candidates who threaten to capture nominations. Kerry, Edwards, and other candidates began attacking Dean's record and electability, arguing that his liberal positions and passionate rhetoric would make him vulnerable to Republican attacks in a general election.

"Once Howard became the frontrunner, everyone started shooting at him," recalled Dean's communications director Tricia Enright. "We went from being the insurgent challenger to being the establishment target, and we weren't prepared for that transition."

Dean's response to his new frontrunner status revealed the limitations that would ultimately constrain his breakthrough. Rather than moderating his rhetoric or building bridges to skeptical Democrats, he often became more combative and defensive. His tendency to respond to criticism with sharper attacks on his opponents made him appear angry and unstable rather than presidential and unifying.

Dean's breakthrough campaign was built on a fundamental contradiction that would ultimately contribute to its collapse: the grassroots energy and internet innovation that had powered his rise were difficult to integrate with the professional campaign management that presidential candidates require. His campaign organization struggled to balance the spontaneous activism of his online supporters with the disciplined messaging and strategic coordination that successful campaigns demand.

The tension was particularly evident in Iowa, where Dean's internet-driven campaign had attracted thousands of enthusiastic supporters from outside the state who volunteered to help with his caucus operation. While this influx of volunteers demonstrated the passion that Dean's candidacy had generated, many of these supporters were unfamiliar with Iowa's political culture and inadvertently reinforced perceptions that Dean represented an invasion of outsiders rather than a grassroots Iowa movement.

"We had incredible energy and enthusiasm, but we struggled to channel that energy into effective political action," acknowledged Dean's Iowa coordinator Sarah Leonard. "Our volunteers were passionate about Howard, but passion alone doesn't win caucuses if you don't understand how the process works."

Dean's campaign also suffered from management problems that reflected the rapid growth it had experienced throughout 2003. The organization that had been perfectly sized for an insurgent candidacy struggled to handle the logistical demands that came with frontrunner status. Internal conflicts between traditional political operatives and internet innovators created strategic confusion and tactical mistakes.

The campaign's rapid expansion also strained its financial resources in ways that were not immediately apparent to outside observers. Despite Dean's impressive fundraising totals, his campaign was spending money faster than it was raising it, creating budget pressures that forced difficult decisions about resource allocation in the crucial final weeks before Iowa.

Dean's collapse in Iowa on January 19, 2004, represented one of the most dramatic reversals of fortune in modern political history. Polls taken just weeks before the caucuses had shown him with a commanding lead, yet he finished third with just 18 percent of the vote, behind both Kerry (38 percent) and Edwards (32 percent) in a result that stunned even his harshest critics.

The Iowa defeat was particularly devastating because it occurred in a state where Dean's campaign had invested enormous resources and had built what appeared to be a formidable organization. His failure there suggested that his internet-driven grassroots support had not translated into the kind of traditional political organizing that Iowa's caucus system required.

Exit polls revealed the narrowness of Dean's coalition, which was concentrated among college-educated liberals who were passionate about his anti-war message but who constituted a minority of Democratic caucus participants. His campaign had failed to build significant support among working-class Democrats, older voters, and moderate Democrats who formed crucial parts of the state's Democratic electorate.

"Iowa showed that our internet success hadn't translated into the kind of broad coalition that you need to win Democratic primaries," reflected Trippi. "We had created an echo chamber of people who shared our views, but we hadn't figured out how to appeal to Democrats who didn't already agree with us."

The Iowa result also revealed the limitations of Dean's anti-establishment message in a contest where electability against Bush was a primary concern for many voters. His opponents had successfully argued that his liberal positions and combative style would make him vulnerable in a general election, a message that resonated with Iowa Democrats who prioritized defeating Bush over ideological purity.

Dean's post-Iowa speech at the Val-Air Ballroom was intended to rally his demoralized supporters and demonstrate that his campaign would continue despite the disappointing results. Instead, it became a political disaster that overshadowed everything else about his candidacy and effectively ended his presidential ambitions.

The speech itself was not particularly unusual by the standards of political rallies. Dean was simply trying to energize his supporters by promising to continue campaigning in the upcoming primary states. However, the combination of his hoarse voice, the crowd's loud response, and the campaign's failure to provide television networks with proper audio created a clip that made Dean appear unhinged and unpresidential.

"The scream was really about technical problems and media coverage rather than anything Howard actually did wrong," observed political journalist Walter Shapiro, who was present at the event. "But once that clip started being replayed on television, it didn't matter what the context had been. Howard looked crazy, and in presidential politics, looking crazy is usually fatal."

The media's obsession with the Dean Scream reflected the kind of pack journalism that can destroy political candidacies in the modern media environment. Television networks replayed the clip hundreds of times, often without providing context about the crowd noise that had prompted Dean's enthusiastic response. Late-night comedy shows used the clip to mock Dean's candidacy, reinforcing perceptions that he was temperamentally unsuited for the presidency.

More damagingly, the intense focus on Dean's emotional outburst distracted attention from his policy positions and his campaign's innovations, reducing his candidacy to a single moment of perceived instability. Voters who might have been attracted to his anti-war message or his use of internet technology instead focused on questions about his judgment and emotional control.

Dean's defeat in New Hampshire on January 27, 2004, confirmed that his Iowa collapse had been more than just a tactical setback—it represented the complete breakdown of his insurgent campaign. His second-place finish, with just 26 percent of the vote to Kerry's 38 percent, occurred in a state where he had been leading by double digits just weeks earlier.

The New Hampshire result was particularly devastating because it occurred in a state that should have been ideal for Dean's insurgency. New Hampshire's independent-minded voters and its tradition of supporting anti-establishment candidates had seemed perfectly suited to Dean's anti-war message and his criticism of Democratic Party orthodoxy.

Dean's New Hampshire campaign also revealed how quickly political momentum could dissipate when breakthrough candidates encountered sustained negative coverage. The media narrative that had once portrayed Dean as the most innovative and exciting candidate in the race suddenly focused on his electoral vulnerabilities and his apparent inability to handle the pressures of frontrunner status.

"New Hampshire showed that once you're perceived as a loser, it becomes almost impossible to change that perception," acknowledged O'Connor. "Howard went from being the candidate of change to being the candidate who couldn't handle change."

The New Hampshire defeat also demonstrated the limitations of Dean's internet-driven campaign model when it encountered traditional political realities. His online supporters remained passionate and committed, but their enthusiasm could not overcome the fundamental problems that had been revealed in Iowa: a narrow coalition, organizational weaknesses, and a candidate who struggled with the scrutiny that comes with national political prominence.

Dean officially withdrew from the presidential race on February 18, 2004, acknowledging that his campaign could not recover from its early defeats and that continuing would only harm the Democratic Party's chances of defeating Bush. His withdrawal speech captured both the disappointment of his supporters and his understanding that his campaign had achieved something significant despite its electoral failure.

"We have transformed the Democratic Party," Dean declared in his withdrawal speech. "We have brought new people into the political process, we have shown that ordinary Americans can challenge the special interests, and we have proven that the internet can be a powerful tool for democratic participation."

Dean's assessment was largely accurate. His campaign had indeed revolutionized political fundraising and organizing, demonstrating how internet technologies could be used to build grassroots support and collect small-dollar contributions. His innovations would be adopted by virtually every subsequent presidential campaign, fundamentally altering how American politics is conducted.

More importantly, Dean's campaign had mobilized hundreds of thousands of Americans who had previously been disconnected from the political process. His Meetup groups and online communities had created networks of political activists who would remain engaged in Democratic politics long after his candidacy ended.

Dean's 2004 breakthrough illustrated both the potential and the pitfalls of technological innovation in political campaigns. His pioneering use of the internet had enabled him to build a national organization and raise millions of dollars despite starting the race as an unknown candidate with minimal establishment support. Yet the same technologies that had powered his rise had also created vulnerabilities that his opponents and the media were able to exploit.

The campaign's reliance on internet-based organizing had created an echo chamber effect that may have insulated Dean and his advisers from feedback that might have helped them adjust their strategy. The passionate online community that surrounded Dean's candidacy had reinforced his anti-establishment message while providing little insight into how that message was being received by Democrats who were not already committed to his cause.

"The internet gave us incredible capabilities, but it also created blind spots," reflected Trippi years later. "We could see our own supporters very clearly, but we had trouble understanding what other Democrats were thinking. That probably contributed to our strategic mistakes."

Dean's breakthrough also revealed the double-edged nature of media coverage in the Internet age. The same digital technologies that had allowed his campaign to generate enormous grassroots support had also made it easier for negative coverage to spread rapidly and widely. The Dean Scream became a viral phenomenon precisely because internet technologies made it easy to share and discuss political content.

Despite Dean's electoral failure, his campaign's innovations proved remarkably sustainable, influencing American political campaigns for decades after his withdrawal. Barack Obama's 2008 presidential campaign built directly on Dean's internet organizing model, using social media and online fundraising to create an even more sophisticated grassroots operation. Subsequent campaigns by candidates in both parties adopted variations of Dean's approach to small-dollar fundraising and digital organizing.

Dean himself remained a significant figure in Democratic politics, serving as chairman of the Democratic National Committee from 2005 to 2009 and helping to rebuild the party's organizational capacity in red states through his "50-State Strategy." His influence on Democratic politics extended far beyond his presidential campaign, shaping the party's approach to grassroots organizing and candidate recruitment.

"Howard's real legacy wasn't his presidential campaign—it was what his innovations made possible for other candidates," observed Democratic strategist Donna Brazile. "He showed that you could build a national political movement from the grassroots up, using technology to connect people who shared common goals."

Dean's breakthrough and collapse served as a cautionary tale about the challenges facing candidates who attempt to revolutionize political campaigning while simultaneously running for the nation's highest office. His campaign demonstrated that innovation alone was insufficient for political success if it was not combined with traditional political skills like coalition-building, message discipline, and strategic patience.

The Dean campaign also revealed the dangers of becoming too identified with a single technological or strategic innovation. Dean's association with internet campaigning, while initially an asset, became a liability when critics portrayed his online support as somehow less authentic or legitimate than traditional political organizing.

Perhaps most importantly, Dean's experience illustrated the difficulty of managing the transition from insurgent challenger to established frontrunner. His campaign had excelled at the breakthrough phase of presidential politics but had struggled with the sustainability challenges that successful campaigns must navigate.

"Howard's campaign was a classic shooting star," observed political scientist Kathleen Hall Jamieson. "It burned brightly and inspired a lot of people, but it couldn't sustain itself once it encountered the full pressure of presidential politics. That doesn't diminish what it accomplished, but it does show the difference between innovation and election."

Howard Dean's 2004 breakthrough stands as one of the most influential failed campaigns in American political history. His innovations in internet organizing and small-dollar fundraising fundamentally changed how presidential campaigns are conducted, while his passionate anti-war message helped establish the liberal activism that would eventually propel Barack Obama to the presidency.

Yet Dean's ultimate failure also demonstrated the limitations facing candidates who attempt to build presidential campaigns around technological innovation rather than traditional political coalition-building. His ability to harness new technologies and tap into voter anger had enabled him to break through the crowded field of Democratic candidates, but it had not prepared him for the sustained scrutiny and organized opposition that frontrunner status inevitably brings.

The tragedy of Dean's breakthrough was not that he failed—most insurgent candidates do—but that his obvious talents for innovation and political mobilization were never fully integrated with the strategic discipline and tactical flexibility that presidential success requires. He had shown that American politics remained open to revolutionary change, but he had also shown that revolution was not enough if it was not accompanied by the kind of political craftsmanship that transforms movements into governing coalitions.

The doctor from Vermont had prescribed the right medicine for a Democratic Party that needed technological modernization and grassroots energy. But his inability to manage his own political symptoms—the anger, the combativeness, the isolation from traditional sources of political wisdom—had prevented him from administering that medicine to a patient who desperately needed healing. His scream had ended his candidacy, but his innovations would echo through American politics for generations to come.

“Obama’s ability to mobilize young voters, African Americans, and college-educated professionals created a coalition that would reshape Democratic politics for the next decade.”

12

OBAMA PHENOMENON (2008)

The crowd inside the Hy-Vee Hall in Des Moines was unlike anything veteran political reporters had witnessed at a campaign rally. More than 4,000 people packed the venue on a humid July evening in 2007, with hundreds more waiting outside unable to get in. The audience was strikingly diverse—not just racially, though that was remarkable enough for an Iowa political event, but generationally and economically. College students sat next to senior citizens, union workers alongside young professionals, longtime Democratic activists beside people who had never attended a political event in their lives.

"We are not red states and blue states—we are the United States of America!" Barack Obama declared from the stage, his voice carrying clearly to the far reaches of the hall without amplification. The crowd erupted, but this was different from the usual political theater of orchestrated applause. This felt spontaneous, authentic, transformative—as if the people in that room genuinely believed they were witnessing the beginning of something that could change American politics forever.

Standing at the back of the hall, David Plouffe, Obama's campaign manager, allowed himself a moment of quiet satisfaction. For months, the political establishment had dismissed Obama's candidacy as premature at best, delusional at worst. Hillary Clinton was the inevitable Democratic nominee, they said, with her superior organization, fundraising apparatus, and political experience. Obama was an inspirational speaker, perhaps, but not a serious presidential candidate.

Yet as Plouffe surveyed the electric crowd and watched Obama work the rope line afterward, signing autographs and taking selfies with supporters who treated him more like a rock star than a politician, he knew something extraordinary was happening. The question was whether

Obama's undeniable ability to inspire could be translated into the kind of systematic political operation that could actually win the Democratic nomination and the presidency.

Less than six months later, Obama would answer that question definitively with his victory in the Iowa caucuses—a breakthrough that would launch one of the most remarkable presidential campaigns in American history and prove that in the right circumstances, with the right candidate and the right strategy, breakthrough moments could indeed be sustained all the way to the White House.

Barack Obama's path to the 2008 presidential race had been meteoric by any conventional measure, yet his decision to challenge Hillary Clinton seemed to defy political logic. A first-term senator with less than four years of national political experience, Obama possessed none of the traditional credentials that presidential candidates typically accumulated over decades of public service.

What Obama did possess was something rarer and more valuable: the ability to articulate a vision of American politics that transcended the partisan divisions and cultural conflicts that had defined the nation's political discourse since the 1960s. His 2004 keynote address at the Democratic National Convention had introduced him to a national audience as a different kind of political leader—one who could speak about controversial subjects without seeming divisive, who could inspire hope without appearing naive.

"Barack had this unique ability to make people believe that politics could be about bringing out the best in America rather than exploiting our worst instincts," recalled David Axelrod, Obama's chief strategist. "That's a rare gift in any politician, but it was especially powerful in 2008 when people were exhausted by eight years of divisive politics."

Obama's decision to seek the presidency was driven partly by ambition but mostly by his conviction that the country was ready for a fundamental change in how politics was conducted. The Iraq War, the Hurricane Katrina response, and the growing economic inequality had created a sense that the American political system was broken and needed renewal that went beyond mere policy adjustments.

The challenge for Obama was how to convert his inspirational message into the kind of practical political coalition that could defeat Hillary

Clinton's formidable campaign organization. Clinton possessed every possible advantage: name recognition, fundraising networks, endorsements from elected officials, and the strategic expertise of her husband's political team. She was, by any objective measure, the most qualified and best-positioned candidate for the Democratic nomination.

Obama's breakthrough began with a message that was both simple and revolutionary: "Change We Can Believe In." The slogan captured perfectly the mood of Democratic primary voters who were frustrated not just with Republican policies but with the cautious, poll-tested approach that had characterized their own party's recent campaigns.

What made Obama's change message different from typical political rhetoric was its specificity about the kind of change he was proposing. Rather than simply promising different policies, Obama argued for a different kind of politics—one that would transcend partisan divisions, engage citizens who had become alienated from the political process, and restore America's moral leadership in the world.

"This campaign is not just about changing policies," Obama said in his announcement speech in Springfield, Illinois, standing in front of the Old State Capitol where Abraham Lincoln had served. "It's about changing how we do politics in America. It's about bringing people together around our common hopes instead of dividing them around our petty fears."

The message resonated particularly strongly with younger voters who had come of age during the Bush administration and were hungry for political leadership that reflected their values and aspirations. Obama's campaign attracted volunteers in their twenties and thirties who had never been deeply involved in politics but who were inspired by his vision of what American democracy could become.

Obama's change message was also perfectly calibrated for the moment in Democratic politics. Primary voters were not just looking for a candidate who could defeat John McCain; they wanted someone who could heal the divisions that had plagued American society and restore the sense of common purpose that seemed to have been lost during the Bush years.

What distinguished Obama's 2008 campaign from previous insurgent candidacies was its combination of inspirational messaging with organizational sophistication that rivaled or exceeded that of establishment campaigns. Building on lessons learned from Howard Dean's 2004 breakthrough and collapse, Obama's team understood that revolutionary rhetoric needed to be supported by systematic political operations.

The foundation of Obama's organizational strength was his early investment in states that other campaigns had written off or ignored. While Clinton focused her resources on states she expected to win easily, Obama's campaign quietly built operations in caucus states and Republican-leaning states where superior organization could overcome Clinton's advantages in name recognition and endorsements.

"We studied every single contest and figured out how to maximize our delegate count," explained Plouffe. "Hillary's campaign was running to win big states and get good headlines. We were running to accumulate the delegates we needed for the nomination."

This strategic approach required Obama's campaign to master the complex rules governing Democratic delegate allocation—rules that had been largely ignored by previous insurgent campaigns. Obama's advisers understood that the Democratic Party's proportional representation system meant that even narrow losses could yield significant delegates, while decisive victories in smaller states could provide crucial advantages.

The campaign's organizational sophistication was particularly evident in its approach to voter contact and mobilization. Rather than relying primarily on television advertising and traditional campaign events, Obama's operation emphasized personal contact through canvassing, phone banking, and community organizing techniques adapted for electoral politics.

Obama's campaign represented the maturation of internet-based political organizing, building on Dean's innovations while avoiding the pitfalls that had undermined his breakthrough. Where Dean's internet strategy had sometimes seemed disconnected from traditional political operations, Obama's team integrated online and offline organizing into a seamless political machine.

The centerpiece of Obama's internet strategy was MyBarackObama.com, a social networking platform that allowed supporters to organize events, coordinate volunteer activities, and raise money from their personal networks. The platform enabled the kind of grassroots organizing that had previously required extensive staff coordination, allowing the campaign to scale its operations far beyond what traditional organizing models could have supported.

"The internet allowed us to organize at a level that had never been possible before," recalled Chris Hughes, the Facebook co-founder who managed Obama's online strategy. "We could empower supporters to become organizers in their own communities, creating a distributed network that was both centrally coordinated and locally responsive."

Obama's internet operations also revolutionized political fundraising, collecting hundreds of millions of dollars from small donors who contributed through the campaign's website. This online fundraising provided not just financial resources but also created a massive database of engaged supporters who could be mobilized for volunteer activities and voter contact efforts.

The integration of the internet and traditional organizing was particularly effective in caucus states, where Obama's campaign could use online tools to identify potential supporters and then deploy traditional organizing techniques to ensure they actually participated in the caucus process. This combination proved decisive in Iowa, where Obama's sophisticated organization overcame Clinton's advantages in name recognition and establishment support.

Obama's breakthrough required him to make the same strategic bet that had launched Jimmy Carter's successful 1976 campaign: invest everything in Iowa and hope that victory there would generate momentum for subsequent contests. The decision was risky because failure in Iowa would likely end his candidacy, but success could transform him from an inspirational long-shot into a genuine threat for the nomination.

The Iowa campaign showcased all of Obama's strengths as a candidate and as an organizer. His message of change and unity resonated strongly with Iowa Democratic voters who were tired of partisan conflict and attracted to his promise of a different kind of politics. His personal story as the son of a Kenyan father and a Kansas mother embodied the multicultural America that many Iowa Democrats wanted their country to become.

"Iowa was perfect for Barack because it allowed him to introduce himself to voters personally," recalled Pete Rouse, Obama's Senate chief of staff, who played a crucial role in the early campaign. "His ability to connect with people in small groups, his knowledge of policy details, his obvious sincerity—all of that came through in the intimate settings that Iowa politics requires."

Obama's Iowa organization was built around the community organizing principles he had learned as a young man in Chicago, emphasizing relationship-building and personal contact over traditional political tactics. His field organizers, many of them young and idealistic, spent months building relationships with potential supporters and creating the kind of personal connections that could translate into caucus participation.

The campaign's approach to Iowa also reflected its understanding of how the state's unique political culture could amplify Obama's national message. Iowa Democrats prided themselves on their independence and their willingness to support candidates who challenged conventional wisdom. Obama's insurgent status and his critique of Washington politics played perfectly to these preferences.

Obama's victory in the Iowa caucuses on January 3, 2008, represented one of the most significant breakthrough moments in modern political history. His 38 percent showing, ahead of John Edwards (30 percent) and Hillary Clinton (29 percent), demonstrated that an African American candidate could win in an overwhelmingly white state and that Obama's inspirational message could translate into actual votes.

The Iowa victory was particularly impressive because it occurred despite Clinton's superior resources and organization. Her campaign had assumed that name recognition and establishment support would be sufficient to win Iowa, but Obama's grassroots operation and superior understanding of caucus dynamics had proven more effective at actually turning out supporters.

"Iowa changed everything," Obama declared in his victory speech. "You have done what the cynics said we couldn't do. You have done what the state of New Hampshire can do in five days. You have done what America can do in this new year, 2008."

The victory generated exactly the kind of momentum that breakthrough campaigns require. Television networks devoted extensive coverage to Obama's upset, with reporters analyzing how he had managed to defeat the presumed nominee. Editorial writers across the country praised his victory and speculated about its implications for both the Democratic nomination and American racial politics.

More tangibly, Obama's Iowa victory triggered massive increases in fundraising and volunteer recruitment. His campaign raised $32 million in January 2008, more than any previous candidate had raised in a single month. Volunteers flooded his campaign offices in upcoming primary states, and his organization began attracting experienced political operatives who had previously remained neutral in the race.

What distinguished Obama's breakthrough from those of previous insurgent candidates was his ability to sustain the momentum generated by his Iowa victory across a long and grueling primary campaign. His subsequent victories in South Carolina, Wisconsin, Virginia, and a string of other states demonstrated that his appeal extended far beyond the unique circumstances of Iowa's political culture.

Obama's sustainability was evident in his campaign's ability to adapt to different political environments while maintaining its core message and organizational effectiveness. His South Carolina victory, powered by overwhelming African American support, showed that he could mobilize minority voters. His Wisconsin victory demonstrated his appeal to white working-class voters. His victories in red states like Virginia and North Carolina proved that his message could resonate beyond traditional Democratic strongholds.

"Barack's campaign was remarkable because it kept getting stronger as it went along," observed Democratic strategist Joe Biden, who would later become Obama's running mate. "Most insurgent campaigns peak early and then fade. Barack's campaign hit its stride in Iowa and then maintained that level of performance for months."

The sustainability of Obama's breakthrough was also evident in his campaign's financial operations. His combination of small-dollar online fundraising and traditional high-dollar events generated resources that allowed him to compete with Clinton's superior initial fundraising advantages. By the end of the primary campaign, Obama had raised more money than any candidate in political history.

Perhaps most importantly, Obama's campaign demonstrated remarkable message discipline and strategic consistency throughout the long primary season. While Clinton's campaign went through multiple strategic repositions and message changes, Obama's team maintained its focus on change, unity, and hope even when facing setbacks in states like New Hampshire and Pennsylvania.

Obama's ultimate victory in the Democratic nomination fight demonstrated his campaign's superior understanding of the party's complex delegate allocation rules. While Clinton focused on winning large primary states that generated favorable media coverage, Obama's team systematically accumulated delegates from caucus states and smaller primaries that Clinton had largely ignored.

The delegate strategy required Obama's campaign to compete everywhere rather than concentrating resources on a few must-win states. This approach meant building organizations in states like Alaska, Idaho, and Wyoming that had never received serious attention from presidential campaigns, but where superior organization could yield decisive delegate advantages.

"We understood that the nomination would be won in the delegate count, not in the media narrative," explained Plouffe. "Every delegate mattered, whether it came from California or American Samoa. That discipline allowed us to build an insurmountable lead even when we were losing some of the bigger contests."

Obama's delegate strategy also reflected his campaign's confidence in its organizational abilities. Building operations in fifty states simultaneously required enormous resources and sophisticated coordination, but Obama's combination of online organizing tools and traditional grassroots techniques made such expansion possible.

The delegate mathematics ultimately vindicated Obama's strategic approach. Despite Clinton's victories in large states like New York, California, and Pennsylvania, Obama's consistent performance across all contests gave him the delegate lead that he never relinquished, effectively securing the nomination by early June 2008.

Obama's 2008 breakthrough represented more than just the success of another insurgent candidate—it demonstrated how the right candidate with the right message and the right organization could fundamentally alter American political possibilities. His ability to mobilize young voters, African Americans, and college-educated professionals created a coalition that would reshape Democratic politics for the next decade.

The campaign also revolutionized political communications, using social media platforms like Facebook and Twitter to reach voters directly and create communities of supporters who could organize independently of traditional campaign structures. These innovations would be copied by candidates in both parties and would fundamentally change how political campaigns are conducted.

"Barack's campaign showed that politics could be about inspiring people rather than just persuading them," reflected Axelrod. "He proved that Americans were hungry for leadership that appealed to their better angels rather than their fears and prejudices."

Obama's breakthrough also had profound implications for American racial politics, demonstrating that white voters would support an African American candidate in sufficient numbers to make him president. His success challenged assumptions about the limitations imposed by racial dynamics and created new possibilities for minority candidates at every level of American politics.

Obama's successful transition from breakthrough candidate to president revealed both the potential and the limitations of inspirational politics in the American system. His ability to generate enormous enthusiasm and mobilize passionate supporters had been perfectly suited to campaign politics, but governing required different skills and faced different constraints.

The challenges Obama faced as president—economic recession, partisan polarization, institutional gridlock—proved resistant to the inspirational rhetoric and grassroots organizing that had powered his campaign. His efforts to maintain the "movement" aspect of his political coalition while simultaneously governing as president created tensions that were never fully resolved.

"Campaigning and governing are completely different skill sets," acknowledged one Obama administration official. "Barack was brilliant at inspiring people to believe that change was possible, but actually implementing that change required dealing with political realities that couldn't be overcome through inspiration alone."

Yet Obama's presidency also demonstrated how breakthrough campaigns could be sustained into effective governance when candidates possessed the intellectual capabilities and strategic patience that successful governing requires. His major legislative achievements—healthcare reform, financial regulation, climate change initiatives—showed that inspirational politics could be converted into concrete policy accomplishments.

Obama's 2008 breakthrough established a template for successful insurgent campaigns that would influence American politics for decades. His combination of inspirational messaging, superior organization, technological innovation, and strategic discipline provided a model that future candidates would attempt to emulate.

The Obama model showed that breakthrough campaigns could succeed by building broader and more diverse coalitions than traditional insurgencies had attempted. Rather than appealing primarily to ideological activists or disaffected voters, Obama had constructed a coalition that included both passionate supporters and pragmatic Democrats who simply wanted to win elections.

"Barack proved that you didn't have to choose between inspiring your base and appealing to the center," observed Democratic strategist Jennifer Palmieri, who worked in the Obama administration. "He showed that the right candidate with the right message could expand the electorate in ways that made traditional political calculations obsolete."

Obama's success also demonstrated the importance of combining breakthrough moments with sustained organizational excellence. His Iowa victory had been crucial for establishing his credibility, but his ultimate success had depended on his campaign's ability to maintain its effectiveness across months of intensive competition.

Barack Obama's 2008 breakthrough stands as the most successful insurgent campaign in modern American political history, proving that under the right circumstances, breakthrough moments could indeed be sustained all the way to the presidency. His victory demonstrated that American politics remained open to fundamental change when candidates could offer voters genuine alternatives to conventional approaches.

Obama's campaign also showed how technological innovation, inspirational messaging, and superior organization could combine to overcome even the most formidable establishment advantages. His defeat of Hillary Clinton, despite her superior initial resources and political network, proved that in American democracy, the best-funded candidate was not always the strongest candidate.

Perhaps most importantly, Obama's breakthrough revealed the continuing power of hope and optimism in American politics. His message that "Yes We Can" resonated with millions of Americans who were hungry for political leadership that appealed to their idealism rather than their cynicism.

"Barack's campaign reminded us that politics at its best could be about bringing out the nobility in people rather than exploiting their weaknesses," reflected Axelrod years later. "That's a lesson that goes far beyond any single election or candidate."

The young senator from Illinois had accomplished something that political scientists had considered nearly impossible: he had converted a breakthrough moment into sustained political success that fundamentally altered American politics. His phenomenon had proven that in the right hands, with the right strategy, and at the right moment, shooting stars could indeed become lasting suns that illuminated new political possibilities for generations to come.

Obama had not just won the presidency—he had shown that American democracy remained capable of renewal and that breakthrough politics, when properly executed, could overcome even the most entrenched advantages of political establishments. His success would inspire countless future candidates to believe that they, too, could capture lightning in a bottle and sustain it long enough to change the world.

“The fundamental problem was that Santorum’s coalition, while passionate and committed, was too narrow to constitute a majority within the Republican Party.”

13

SANTORUM SURGE (2012)

The phone call came at 3:17 AM on January 4, 2012, jolting Rick Santorum from his first restful sleep in weeks. On the other end was Matt Strawn, chairman of the Iowa Republican Party, with news that would transform a campaign that had been written off as a vanity project into one of the most improbable comebacks in modern political history.

"Senator," Strawn said, his voice betraying the exhaustion that comes from overseeing a recount that had stretched through the night, "I wanted you to be the first to know. When we finish counting the certified results from all 99 counties, you're going to be declared the winner of the Iowa caucuses."

Santorum sat up in his hotel bed, trying to process what he was hearing. For months, his campaign had been an afterthought in the Republican primary, relegated to the second tier of candidates who seemed to be running more for book deals and cable television contracts than for the presidency. His poll numbers had been stuck in single digits, his fundraising had been anemic, and political reporters had largely ignored his campaign events in favor of covering the better-funded operations of Mitt Romney, Newt Gingrich, and Ron Paul.

Yet through a combination of relentless retail politicking, unwavering conservative principles, and the kind of organizational discipline that thrives in Iowa's unique caucus system, Santorum had achieved something that seemed impossible just weeks earlier: he had defeated the establishment frontrunner and positioned himself as the conservative alternative to Romney that Republican voters had been seeking throughout the primary season.

"Matt," Santorum replied, his voice still hoarse from weeks of campaigning in Iowa's winter cold, "are you absolutely certain about this?"

"Senator," Strawn answered, "you won Iowa by 34 votes. Congratulations."

The narrow victory margin of error in any normal election, but decisive in the media narrative that drives presidential campaigns—would launch Santorum from obscurity to the top tier of Republican candidates and demonstrate once again that in American politics, breakthrough moments could still emerge from the most unlikely circumstances.

Rick Santorum's decision to seek the 2012 Republican nomination seemed quixotic from the moment he announced his candidacy in June 2011. A former senator from Pennsylvania who had lost his 2006 reelection bid by an embarrassing 18-point margin, Santorum possessed none of the traditional assets that successful presidential candidates typically assembled: significant name recognition, substantial fundraising networks, or backing from major Republican donors and interest groups.

What Santorum did possess was something that had become increasingly rare in modern Republican politics: an uncompromising commitment to social conservative principles that had never been moderated for electoral advantage or media approval. Throughout his Senate career, Santorum had been one of the most consistent advocates for traditional family values, restrictions on abortion, and the integration of religious faith into public policy—positions that endeared him to evangelical voters but limited his appeal beyond the Republican base.

"Rick was probably the most authentic conservative in the 2012 field," observed Tony Perkins, president of the Family Research Council. "He didn't just talk about conservative values when it was convenient—he had fought for them throughout his career, even when it cost him politically."

Santorum's authenticity on social issues was matched by his blue-collar economic populism, which distinguished him from other Republican candidates who focused primarily on tax cuts for businesses and wealthy individuals. His background as the descendant of Italian immigrants who had worked in blue-collar western Pennsylvania gave him credibility when discussing the economic anxieties of working-class Americans who had been hurt by trade agreements and industrial decline.

The challenge for Santorum was how to convert his authentic conservative credentials into the kind of political support that could overcome his numerous disadvantages in organization, fundraising, and media attention. His campaign began with virtually no institutional support and operated on a shoestring budget that limited his ability to compete in expensive media markets or build the kind of professional organizations that modern presidential campaigns require.

Santorum's breakthrough began with a strategic decision that reflected both necessity and insight: he would concentrate virtually all of his limited resources on Iowa, betting everything on his ability to connect with the state's large population of evangelical voters and social conservatives. The strategy was risky because failure in Iowa would likely end his campaign, but success could provide the momentum and credibility needed to compete in subsequent contests.

The Iowa-first strategy played to Santorum's strengths as a retail politician who excelled in the kind of intimate, personal campaigning that Iowa's political culture rewarded. Unlike television advertising or mass rallies, which required substantial financial resources, retail politics demanded only time, energy, and the ability to connect with voters on a personal level—assets that Santorum possessed in abundance.

"Rick understood that Iowa was his only shot," recalled John Brabender, Santorum's senior strategist. "He couldn't compete with Romney on money or organization, but he could outwork everyone in Iowa and build the personal relationships that caucus politics requires."

Santorum's approach to Iowa was systematic and comprehensive. He visited all 99 counties in the state, often driving himself between events in a rented pickup truck that became a symbol of his grassroots, authentic approach to campaigning. He attended every forum, every debate, and every candidate event that would accept him, using each opportunity to refine his message and build name recognition among Iowa Republicans.

The strategy also reflected Santorum's understanding of Iowa's unique political dynamics. The state's Republican caucus-goers were disproportionately evangelical and socially conservative, exactly the constituency that was most likely to respond to his message about moral values and traditional family structures. His opposition to abortion and same-sex marriage, which might have been liabilities in more moderate states, became assets in Iowa's conservative political environment.

What distinguished Santorum from other candidates competing for conservative support was his ability to articulate social conservative positions with intellectual sophistication and personal conviction rather than political calculation. His arguments against abortion were grounded in philosophical principles about human dignity and the sanctity of life. His opposition to same-sex marriage was presented as part of a broader concern about the breakdown of traditional family structures and their impact on society.

"Rick could talk about social issues in ways that didn't sound like he was pandering to religious voters," observed Ralph Reed, founder of the Christian Coalition. "He had thought deeply about these issues and could explain his positions in ways that appealed to people's minds as well as their hearts."

Santorum's authenticity was particularly evident when he discussed his personal experiences with family tragedy and faith. His decision to continue a pregnancy despite doctors' recommendations after learning that his son Gabriel would likely die shortly after birth, and his family's decision to bring the baby home briefly before his death, provided powerful personal testimony about his pro-life convictions.

These personal stories resonated strongly with evangelical voters who had grown skeptical of politicians who seemed to adopt conservative positions only during campaign seasons. Santorum's willingness to discuss difficult personal experiences and his obvious emotional connection to social issues convinced many conservative voters that his positions were matters of genuine conviction rather than political expediency.

The authenticity extended to Santorum's economic message, which combined traditional conservative positions on taxes and regulation with populist criticisms of trade agreements and corporate policies that had hurt working-class Americans. His background in Pennsylvania's declining industrial regions gave him credibility when discussing the impact of factory closings and job losses on blue-collar families.

Despite his campaign's limited financial resources, Santorum managed to build a surprisingly effective grassroots organization in Iowa through a combination of volunteer enthusiasm and strategic targeting.

His campaign identified the most committed conservative activists in each county and recruited them to serve as local coordinators who could mobilize their networks on caucus night.

The organization was built around personal relationships rather than paid staff or expensive technology. Santorum's county coordinators were typically individuals who had met the candidate personally during his visits to their communities and had been impressed by his authenticity and commitment to conservative principles. These volunteers provided the kind of passionate advocacy that money could not buy.

"Rick's Iowa organization was unlike anything I had seen in modern politics," observed Craig Robinson, a Republican strategist who covered the Iowa caucuses extensively. "It was held together by personal relationships and shared beliefs rather than professional campaign management. That made it incredibly effective at the grassroots level."

The grassroots approach also allowed Santorum's campaign to compete effectively in Iowa's unique caucus system, which required intensive organization and personal persuasion rather than the mass communication strategies that dominated primary elections. His supporters were trained to argue for their candidate in the face-to-face discussions that characterize Iowa caucuses, and their passion and knowledge often proved more persuasive than the talking points distributed by better-funded campaigns.

Santorum's organization also benefited from the support of influential social conservative leaders who had remained neutral in the race but privately encouraged their followers to consider supporting his candidacy. These informal endorsements provided Santorum with access to the networks of evangelical churches, home-school groups, and pro-life organizations that formed the backbone of Iowa's conservative movement.

Santorum's breakthrough began in earnest during the final weeks before the Iowa caucuses, when his combination of authentic conservative messaging and relentless retail campaigning began generating the kind of momentum that characterizes successful insurgent campaigns. His poll numbers, which had been mired in single digits throughout 2011, began climbing steadily as Iowa Republicans took a closer look at his candidacy.

The surge was powered by several factors that converged in Santorum's favor during Iowa's final month. First, conservative voters who had been shopping for alternatives to Romney finally began coalescing around

Santorum as the most credible conservative candidate in the race. Second, his strong performances in Iowa debates and candidate forums generated positive media coverage that improved his name recognition and credibility.

Most importantly, Santorum benefited from the collapse of other candidates who had briefly led in Iowa polls. Herman Cain's campaign imploded amid personal scandals, while Newt Gingrich's surge dissipated under attack ads funded by Romney's super PAC. These developments cleared the field for Santorum to emerge as the principal conservative alternative to Romney.

"Rick was in the right place at the right time," acknowledged Gingrich strategist Joe DeSantis. "Conservative voters had been looking for someone they could trust, and Rick's authenticity and consistency finally broke through when other candidates faltered."

The late surge also reflected the effectiveness of Santorum's Iowa strategy. His months of county visits and personal campaigning had built a foundation of support that became visible only when conservative voters began paying close attention to the race. His grassroots organization provided the infrastructure needed to convert growing interest into actual caucus participation.

Santorum's narrow victory in the Iowa caucuses represented one of the most stunning upsets in Republican primary history. His 25 percent showing, just 34 votes ahead of Romney's 24.6 percent, transformed him overnight from an afterthought into a serious contender for the Republican nomination and demonstrated that authentic conservative messaging could still triumph over superior organization and financial resources.

The victory was particularly impressive because it occurred despite Romney's significant advantages in paid advertising and professional organization. The former Massachusetts governor had spent heavily in Iowa and had built a sophisticated operation designed to identify and mobilize his supporters. Yet Santorum's grassroots campaign and authentic conservative message had proven more effective at actually persuading Iowa Republicans to support his candidacy.

"Iowa proved that money and organization aren't everything in politics," Santorum declared in his victory speech. "When you have a message that resonates with people's values and concerns, when you're willing to work hard and connect with voters personally, you can overcome any disadvantage."

The Iowa victory generated exactly the kind of national media attention that breakthrough campaigns require. Television networks devoted extensive coverage to Santorum's upset, with reporters analyzing how he had managed to defeat better-funded opponents through sheer determination and conservative authenticity. Editorial writers across the country speculated about the implications of his victory for both the Republican nomination and the general election.

More tangibly, Santorum's Iowa breakthrough triggered immediate improvements in his campaign's organizational and financial position. His fundraising increased dramatically in the days following his victory, as conservative donors who had been supporting other candidates began switching their allegiances to the candidate who had proven he could win.

Despite his Iowa breakthrough, Santorum faced the same challenge that had confronted other insurgent candidates: how to translate initial success into the kind of sustained campaign that could compete effectively across multiple states with different political cultures and organizational requirements. His victory in Iowa had been achieved through a strategy that was perfectly suited to that state's unique circumstances but might not be replicable elsewhere.

The immediate challenge was New Hampshire, where Santorum's social conservative message was less likely to resonate with the state's more libertarian-minded Republican electorate. His campaign lacked the financial resources and organizational infrastructure to compete effectively in a state that required expensive television advertising and professional campaign operations.

"Iowa and New Hampshire are completely different political environments," acknowledged Santorum strategist John Yob. "What worked for us in Iowa—the personal campaigning, the social conservative message—wasn't necessarily going to work in New Hampshire, where voters are more focused on economic issues and fiscal conservatism."

Santorum's campaign also struggled with the logistical challenges that confront all breakthrough candidacies when they suddenly receive national attention. His small staff was overwhelmed by media requests, speaking invitations, and the complex scheduling demands that come with front-runner status. The campaign that had been perfectly sized for Iowa's retail politics was unprepared for the demands of a national campaign.

More problematically, Santorum discovered that his Iowa breakthrough had attracted the kind of scrutiny from opponents and media that had previously been focused on other candidates. His record as a senator, his positions on social issues, and his electability in a general election all became subjects of intense examination that his campaign was not prepared to handle.

Santorum's momentum appeared to dissipate with his fifth-place finish in New Hampshire on January 10, 2012, where his 9 percent showing seemed to confirm that his Iowa victory had been more of a regional anomaly than evidence of broad conservative support. The New Hampshire result raised questions about whether his breakthrough could be sustained in states where his social conservative message was less central to Republican primary politics.

However, Santorum demonstrated the resilience that characterizes successful breakthrough campaigns by reviving his candidacy in South Carolina, where his social conservative message and blue-collar background resonated more strongly with the state's Republican electorate. His strong performances in South Carolina debates and his passionate defense of conservative principles helped him recover from his New Hampshire disappointment.

The South Carolina campaign also revealed Santorum's ability to adapt his message to different political environments while maintaining his core conservative appeal. In a state with significant military presence and foreign policy concerns, he emphasized his experience with national security issues and his support for strong defense policies. In a state with significant economic anxiety, he highlighted his proposals for manufacturing jobs and his criticism of trade policies that had hurt American workers.

"South Carolina showed that Rick could compete outside of Iowa if he could get his message across," observed Republican strategist Katon Dawson. "His problem wasn't that his appeal was too narrow—it was that he lacked the resources to communicate effectively in multiple states simultaneously."

Santorum's third-place finish in South Carolina, with 17 percent of the vote, was disappointing but sufficient to keep his campaign viable and position him for stronger performances in upcoming contests where his message might resonate more effectively.

Santorum's most impressive breakthrough period came in February 2012, when he won three contests in a single day—the Minnesota and Colorado caucuses and the Missouri primary—demonstrating that his Iowa victory had not been a fluke and that his conservative message could attract support across different regions and demographic groups.

The February 7 victories were particularly significant because they occurred in states with very different political cultures and economic circumstances. Minnesota's Republican caucus-goers were heavily evangelical and socially conservative, similar to Iowa's electorate. Colorado's Republicans were more diverse economically and geographically, including significant numbers of suburban professionals and rural conservatives. Missouri's primary electorate was influenced by the state's urban-rural divide and its complex racial and economic dynamics.

"The February sweep proved that Rick had built a genuine conservative movement rather than just an Iowa-specific campaign," reflected Brabender. "He was connecting with Republican voters who wanted an authentic conservative alternative to Romney, regardless of where they lived."

The victories also demonstrated Santorum's superior understanding of caucus dynamics and his campaign's ability to mobilize passionate supporters in low-turnout contests. His grassroots organization, while limited in resources, was effective at identifying and turning out the most committed conservative activists—exactly the kinds of voters who were most likely to participate in caucuses and non-binding primaries.

The February breakthrough generated renewed media attention and fundraising for Santorum's campaign, allowing him to expand his operations and compete more effectively in upcoming primary states. His ability to win multiple contests in a single day forced Republican voters and party leaders to take his candidacy seriously as a potential alternative to Romney's establishment campaign.

Despite his impressive February victories, Santorum's campaign ultimately encountered the organizational and strategic limitations that constrain most breakthrough candidacies. His success in caucus states and low-turnout contests, while impressive, did not translate effectively to the large primary states that would ultimately determine the Republican nomination.

The fundamental problem was that Santorum's coalition, while passionate and committed, was too narrow to constitute a majority within the Republican Party. His appeal was concentrated among evangelical voters and social conservatives who formed important parts of the party's base but who were insufficient for sustained success in a diverse national campaign.

"Rick's ceiling was probably around 35-40 percent of Republican primary voters," acknowledged one Santorum adviser years later. "That was enough to win in certain circumstances, but it wasn't enough to actually secure the nomination once the field narrowed and other candidates consolidated opposition to his candidacy."

Santorum's campaign also struggled with the financial and organizational demands of competing in multiple large states simultaneously. His breakthrough victories had improved his fundraising, but he remained significantly outspent by Romney's campaign and its allied super PACs. His organization, while effective in caucus states, lacked the professional infrastructure needed for expensive primary contests in states like Florida, New York, and California.

Perhaps most importantly, Santorum never successfully made the transition from insurgent challenger to credible general election candidate. His strong conservative positions, while authentic and appealing to Republican primary voters, raised questions about his ability to attract the independent and moderate voters who typically determine presidential elections.

Santorum officially suspended his presidential campaign on April 10, 2012, acknowledging that Romney had effectively secured the Republican nomination and that continuing his campaign would only divide the party heading into the general election. His withdrawal speech captured both the accomplishment and the limitations of his breakthrough campaign.

"We made a difference in this race," Santorum declared. "We showed that a campaign built on conservative principles and grassroots activism could compete with the most well-funded political operations in the country. We proved that authenticity and hard work still matter in American politics."

Santorum's assessment was largely accurate. His campaign had indeed demonstrated that breakthrough moments remained possible for candidates who combined authentic messaging with strategic discipline and relentless effort. His victories in eleven states and his accumulation of nearly 300 delegates represented a remarkable achievement for a campaign that had begun with virtually no institutional support.

More importantly, Santorum's breakthrough had influenced the direction of Republican politics by demonstrating the continued strength of social conservative activism within the party. His success had forced Romney to adopt more conservative positions on social issues and had shown that candidates who ignored the party's evangelical base did so at their own peril.

Santorum's 2012 breakthrough was significant not just for its electoral success but for its demonstration that conservative politics could appeal to working-class voters who had been increasingly alienated from both major political parties. His combination of social conservatism and economic populism provided a template for Republican candidates seeking to build coalitions that extended beyond the party's traditional base of affluent suburbanites and business interests.

"Rick showed that there was a constituency for a different kind of conservatism," observed Yuval Levin, editor of National Affairs. "His appeal to working-class voters who shared conservative values but were skeptical of corporate capitalism pointed toward political realignments that wouldn't be fully realized until Donald Trump's 2016 campaign."

Santorum's emphasis on manufacturing jobs, his criticism of trade agreements that had hurt American workers, and his defense of traditional communities under economic pressure would all become central themes in Republican politics during the Trump era. His breakthrough had identified important constituencies and messages that would reshape conservative politics in subsequent election cycles.

Rick Santorum's 2012 breakthrough stands as one of the most impressive insurgent campaigns in modern Republican primary history, demonstrating that authentic conservative messaging combined with strategic discipline and relentless effort could overcome enormous disadvantages in organization and financial resources. His victory in Iowa and his subsequent wins in ten additional states proved that breakthrough moments remained possible for candidates who truly understood their party's base voters.

Yet Santorum's ultimate failure to secure the nomination also revealed the persistent limitations facing candidates whose appeal is concentrated among ideological activists rather than broader coalitions. His inability to expand his support beyond committed social conservatives ultimately prevented him from building the kind of majority coalition that successful presidential campaigns require.

The tragedy of Santorum's breakthrough was not that he lost—most insurgent candidates do—but that his obvious talents for authentic conservative messaging and grassroots organizing were never fully integrated with the strategic flexibility and coalition-building skills that sustained political success requires. He had shown that the Republican Party remained responsive to authentic conservative appeals, but he had also shown that authenticity alone was insufficient for lasting political success.

The senator from Pennsylvania had accomplished something remarkable: he had converted a vanity campaign into a genuine threat for the Republican nomination through sheer determination and conservative authenticity. His surge had reminded Republicans that their party's strength lay not in corporate boardrooms or Washington think tanks but in the churches, small towns, and working-class communities where conservative values remained vibrant and politically powerful.

Rick Santorum had proven that in American politics, breakthrough moments could still emerge from the most unlikely circumstances when candidates possessed the courage to speak authentic truths and the discipline to organize effectively around those truths. His shooting star had burned brightly across the Republican firmament, illuminating possibilities for conservative politics that would influence American elections for years to come.

“Trump’s capture of the Republican nomination constituted a hostile takeover of the Republican Party by forces that had been building within the conservative movement for decades.”

14

TRUMP TIDAL WAVE (2016)

The escalator at Trump Tower descended slowly, dramatically, as if choreographed for maximum theatrical effect. At exactly 11:00 AM on June 16, 2015, Donald J. Trump emerged at the bottom, flanked by his wife, Melania, to address a crowd of reporters and paid supporters who had gathered in the marble-and-gold atrium of his Manhattan headquarters.

What followed was unlike any presidential announcement in modern American history. For forty-five minutes, Trump delivered a rambling, improvised speech that violated every rule of conventional political communication. He called Mexican immigrants "rapists" and drug dealers. He boasted about his wealth and business success. He promised to build a wall along the southern border and make Mexico pay for it. He declared that politicians were "stupid" and that only he could fix America's problems.

"We need a leader who wrote 'The Art of the Deal,'" Trump proclaimed, referring to his 1987 bestseller. "We need a leader who can bring back our jobs, can bring back our manufacturing, can bring back our military, and can take care of our vets. We need somebody who literally will take this country and make it great again."

Political reporters in the audience exchanged knowing glances. This was clearly the vanity campaign of a reality television star seeking publicity for his brand rather than a serious presidential candidacy. The speech was too erratic, too offensive, too obviously unscripted to represent genuine political ambition. Trump lacked government experience, policy knowledge, and the organizational infrastructure that serious campaigns required. His announcement would provide entertainment value for a few news cycles before fading into irrelevance.

They could not have been more wrong. Within weeks, Trump would surge to the top of Republican primary polls and remain there for the duration of the campaign. His unconventional approach to politics, rather than disqualifying him, would prove to be exactly what Republican primary voters had been waiting for. His breakthrough would not only capture the Republican nomination but would fundamentally transform American politics, proving that in the right circumstances, the most unlikely candidates could achieve the most unlikely victories.

Donald Trump's decision to seek the presidency represented the culmination of a decades-long flirtation with political ambition that had never been taken seriously by political professionals. The son of a successful New York real estate developer, Trump had built his own business empire in Manhattan while simultaneously creating a public persona as the embodiment of American success and celebrity culture.

Trump's political credentials were virtually nonexistent by traditional standards. He had never held elected office, never managed a government agency, never served in the military. His policy positions were often contradictory or nonexistent, changing based on his audience or his mood. His personal behavior—the multiple divorces, the controversial business practices, the inflammatory statements—seemed to disqualify him from serious political consideration.

Yet Trump possessed assets that traditional politicians lacked: unparalleled name recognition, complete financial independence, and an intuitive understanding of media dynamics that he had developed through decades of courting publicity. His reality television show, "The Apprentice," had reinforced his image as a decisive leader who could solve complex problems, while his active presence on social media had given him direct access to millions of Americans without the filter of traditional news organizations.

"Trump understood that politics had become a form of entertainment," observed Republican strategist Steve Schmidt. "He didn't need to learn how to be a politician—he just needed to apply the skills he had developed as an entertainer and media personality to the political arena."

Trump's political persona was built around his image as a successful businessman who could bring private sector efficiency to government operations. His wealth provided credibility with voters who associated financial success with competence, while his outsider status appealed to

Americans who were frustrated with professional politicians and their perceived failures.

More importantly, Trump possessed something that few political candidates could claim: complete authenticity. His offensive comments, his bragging, his attacks on opponents—all of this was consistent with the public persona he had cultivated for decades. Unlike typical politicians who carefully crafted their images for public consumption, Trump presented himself as he actually was, creating a sense of authenticity that resonated with voters who were tired of scripted, focus-grouped political communication.

Trump's breakthrough was powered by a political message that tapped into deep currents of dissatisfaction that had been building within the Republican Party and American politics more generally. His campaign theme, "Make America Great Again," implied that the country had declined under the leadership of both Democratic and Republican politicians, creating an opening for an outsider who could restore America's strength and prosperity.

The message resonated because it provided a simple explanation for complex problems that many Americans were experiencing: economic stagnation, cultural change, international instability, and the sense that traditional American values were under assault. Rather than offering detailed policy prescriptions, Trump promised to use his business expertise and negotiating skills to solve problems that career politicians had been unable to address.

"Trump's genius was understanding that Republican voters weren't looking for conservative ideology—they were looking for someone who would fight for them," observed pollster Kellyanne Conway, who would later manage Trump's general election campaign. "His message wasn't about policy details—it was about strength, winning, and putting America first."

Trump's anti-establishment message was particularly effective because it allowed him to attack both Democratic policies and Republican leadership with equal fervor. His criticism of trade agreements, military interventions, and immigration policies put him at odds with Republican orthodoxy, but it resonated with working-class voters who felt that both parties had failed to represent their interests.

The message also tapped into cultural anxieties that many Republican voters were experiencing but that few politicians were willing to address directly. Trump's promises to restrict immigration, his criticism of political correctness, and his defense of traditional American culture appealed to voters who felt that their values and way of life were being marginalized by cultural and demographic changes.

What transformed Trump from a novelty candidate into a serious threat was his revolutionary approach to political communication, which bypassed traditional campaign strategies in favor of direct engagement with voters through social media and television appearances. His mastery of Twitter allowed him to set the daily news agenda, respond instantly to critics, and communicate directly with supporters without the filter of mainstream journalism.

Trump's Twitter account became the most powerful weapon in modern political communication, allowing him to break news, attack opponents, and shape public discourse with 280-character messages that generated enormous media coverage. His willingness to tweet controversial statements at any hour of the day created a sense of immediacy and authenticity that traditional political communication could not match.

"Trump turned Twitter into a nuclear weapon," observed political journalist Mark Halperin. "He could destroy opponents, dominate news cycles, and communicate directly with millions of people instantly. No candidate had ever possessed that kind of communication power."

Trump's media strategy also capitalized on the economics of cable television news, which needed compelling content to fill twenty-four hours of programming. His controversial statements and unpredictable behavior provided exactly the kind of dramatic content that television producers craved, ensuring that he received far more coverage than his campaign budget would have allowed him to purchase.

The strategy was particularly effective because it leveraged Trump's decades of experience in attracting media attention. He understood how to create stories that reporters could not ignore, how to use controversy to generate coverage, and how to maintain public attention over sustained periods. His background in reality television had taught him how to create dramatic moments that would capture audience interest and generate discussion.

Trump's campaign rallies became the defining characteristic of his insurgency, creating a form of political theater that had not been seen in American politics since the populist campaigns of the early twentieth century. His rallies were part political event, part entertainment spectacle, part religious revival, generating the kind of passionate enthusiasm that traditional political campaigns struggled to achieve.

The rallies served multiple strategic purposes for Trump's campaign. They provided visual evidence of his popular support, creating images of overflowing crowds that reinforced his claims about his electoral strength. They allowed him to test and refine his political messages, gauging audience reactions to different themes and adjusting his rhetoric accordingly. Most importantly, they created communities of committed supporters who would become volunteers, donors, and advocates for his candidacy.

"The rallies were unlike anything I had ever seen in American politics," observed journalist Salena Zito, who covered many Trump events. "The energy was incredible, the loyalty was intense, and the connection between Trump and his supporters was genuinely emotional. It was clear that something unprecedented was happening."

Trump's rally performances demonstrated his intuitive understanding of mass psychology and his ability to connect with audiences on an emotional rather than intellectual level. His speeches were rarely policy-focused but were always entertaining, combining humor, anger, nostalgia, and hope in ways that kept audiences engaged and enthusiastic.

The rallies also served as effective organizing tools, allowing Trump's campaign to identify and recruit supporters in local communities across the country. Attendees provided contact information that could be used for future mobilization efforts, while the intense experience of attending a Trump rally often converted casual supporters into passionate advocates who would recruit others to his cause.

Trump's dominance of the Republican primary campaign began immediately after his announcement and never wavered despite predictions that his support would eventually collapse. His lead in early polls, initially dismissed as a reflection of his celebrity status rather than genuine political strength, proved remarkably durable throughout the primary season.

The breakthrough was evident in Trump's performance in the first Republican debate on August 6, 2015, where his willingness to attack other candidates and his refusal to pledge support for the eventual Republican nominee dominated post-debate coverage. Rather than hurting his campaign, his controversial debate performance reinforced his image as a different kind of candidate who was willing to challenge political conventions.

Trump's first significant setback came in the Iowa Republican caucuses on February 1, 2016, where he finished second to Ted Cruz with 24.3% of the vote compared to Cruz's 27.6%. Initially, Trump responded with characteristic grace, conceding publicly on caucus night and congratulating Cruz on his victory. "I'm just honored," Trump told supporters. "I want to congratulate Ted, and I want to congratulate all of the incredible candidates."

However, within days, Trump's response revealed a pattern that would become a defining characteristic of his political career: his refusal to accept unfavorable results without challenging their legitimacy. Trump began claiming that Cruz had "stolen" the Iowa caucus through fraudulent means, tweeting that Cruz "didn't win Iowa, he illegally stole it" and calling for either a new election or for Cruz's results to be nullified.

Trump's accusations centered on several alleged irregularities: that Cruz's campaign had spread false rumors about Ben Carson dropping out of the race to redirect Carson supporters to Cruz, that non-residents had voted in the caucuses, and that other unspecified fraudulent activities had occurred. He reportedly even considered pursuing legal action to challenge the results.

"Based on the fraud committed by Senator Ted Cruz during the Iowa Caucus, either a new election should take place or Cruz results should be nullified," Trump tweeted, escalating his claims despite the lack of substantive evidence to support them. Cruz dismissed Trump's accusations as a "temper tantrum," while Iowa GOP officials called the claims absurd and unfounded.

The Iowa episode established a playbook that Trump would return to repeatedly throughout his political career: initial acceptance of adverse results followed by increasingly aggressive challenges to their legitimacy when the initial disappointment transformed into anger and strategic calculation. Rather than damaging his campaign, Trump's willingness to challenge the Iowa results reinforced his image as a fighter who would not accept what he perceived as unfair treatment.

"The debate showed that Trump was playing by different rules," acknowledged Republican strategist Rick Wilson. "While other candidates were trying to appeal to party leaders and demonstrate their qualifications, Trump was appealing directly to voters who wanted someone who would shake up the system."

Trump's subsequent primary victories validated his unconventional approach and demonstrated that his support was not limited to public opinion polls. His wins in New Hampshire, South Carolina, and Nevada showed that he could attract votes across different regions and demographic groups, while his delegate accumulation gave him a mathematical advantage that became increasingly difficult for opponents to overcome.

The primary campaign also revealed the limitations of traditional Republican campaign strategies when confronted with Trump's insurgency. Candidates who had built conventional campaigns based on policy expertise, endorsements, and organized ground operations found themselves unable to compete with Trump's media dominance and populist appeal.

As Trump's primary victories accumulated, the Republican establishment mounted increasingly desperate efforts to derail his candidacy, recognizing that his nomination would represent a fundamental transformation of their party. The counterattack took familiar forms: negative advertising questioning his conservative credentials, warnings about his electability, and attempts to consolidate opposition around alternative candidates.

Yet the establishment attacks often backfired by reinforcing Trump's central campaign theme that he was the outsider candidate who threatened the political system that had failed ordinary Americans. When prominent Republicans criticized his positions or questioned his qualifications, Trump used their opposition as evidence that he was the candidate of change rather than continuity.

"Every time the establishment attacked Trump, it just proved his point about being different," observed Trump adviser Stephen Miller. "Republican voters had lost faith in their party's leadership, so criticism from party leaders was actually an endorsement in the minds of many primary voters."

The establishment's failure to stop Trump reflected their fundamental misunderstanding of the Republican electorate's mood in 2016. Party leaders assumed that voters shared their concerns about Trump's qualifications and temperament, but many Republican primary voters were more interested in choosing a candidate who would challenge the system than one who would manage it competently.

The counterattack also suffered from the fragmentation of opposition to Trump among multiple alternative candidates. Unlike previous establishment efforts to stop insurgent candidates, the anti-Trump movement never consolidated around a single alternative, allowing Trump to win primaries with pluralities while his opponents divided the anti-Trump vote.

Trump's capture of the Republican nomination represented more than just the victory of another insurgent candidate—it constituted a hostile takeover of the Republican Party by forces that had been building within the conservative movement for decades but had never before captured control of the party's presidential nominating process.

The takeover was evident in Trump's ability to win the nomination despite opposition from most Republican elected officials, major donors, and conservative intellectuals. His success demonstrated that the party's base voters were willing to reject the preferences of traditional party leaders in favor of a candidate who promised to represent their interests more directly.

"Trump's nomination showed that the Republican Party had become a populist movement rather than a conservative party," observed political scientist Henry Olsen. "The voters cared more about immigration, trade, and cultural issues than they did about limited government and free markets."

The hostile takeover also revealed the extent to which the Republican Party had been transformed by demographic and ideological changes that party leaders had not fully recognized. Trump's coalition included significant numbers of working-class voters, older Americans, and rural residents who felt alienated from the party's previous emphasis on business interests and suburban professionals.

Trump's nomination acceptance speech at the Republican National Convention in Cleveland captured the transformation he was bringing to the party. His dark portrayal of American decline, his promises to restore law and order, and his explicit appeals to working-class voters represented a dramatic departure from the optimistic, business-friendly message that had characterized Republican politics since the Reagan era.

Trump's most remarkable breakthrough came not in the Republican primaries, where his unconventional campaign had clear advantages, but in the general election, where he faced Hillary Clinton, one of the most experienced and well-prepared candidates in modern political history. His victory demonstrated that the political transformation he represented extended far beyond the Republican Party to include broader changes in American electoral politics.

The general election campaign revealed Trump's ability to maintain his insurgent appeal even after becoming the Republican nominee. His continued attacks on political establishments in both parties, his criticism of media coverage, and his promises to "drain the swamp" in Washington allowed him to present himself as an outsider candidate even while representing a major political party.

"Trump's general election campaign was unprecedented because he ran as an insurgent against the entire political system," observed journalist Matt Taibbi. "He wasn't just running against Hillary Clinton—he was running against politicians, journalists, and institutions that he claimed had failed the American people."

Trump's victory on November 8, 2016, shocked political observers who had dismissed his candidacy from its inception. His ability to win crucial swing states like Pennsylvania, Wisconsin, and Michigan demonstrated that his appeal extended to working-class Democrats who had been reliable parts of their party's coalition for decades.

Unlike most breakthrough candidates, Trump's 2016 success proved remarkably sustainable, not only carrying him to the presidency but fundamentally altering the Republican Party in ways that outlasted his individual candidacy. His transformation of the party from a business-oriented conservative organization into a populist nationalist movement represented a permanent shift rather than a temporary deviation.

Trump's sustainability was evident in his ability to maintain high approval ratings among Republican voters throughout his presidency, despite unprecedented controversy and criticism from traditional party leaders. His hold on the Republican base remained strong even after his

2020 election defeat, demonstrating that his political appeal transcended specific policy achievements or electoral outcomes.

"Trump didn't just win an election—he redefined what it meant to be a Republican," observed conservative commentator Rich Lowry. "His influence on the party was so profound that future Republican candidates would have to adapt to the political world he had created."

The sustainability of Trump's revolution was also evident in the emergence of Trump-aligned candidates throughout the Republican Party who adopted his rhetorical style, policy positions, and political strategies. The 2016 breakthrough had created a new model for Republican politics that influenced campaigns at every level of government.

Trump's 2016 campaign fundamentally altered the relationship between political candidates and news media, demonstrating how social media platforms could be used to bypass traditional journalism and communicate directly with voters. His Twitter account became a more powerful communication tool than any television advertisement or campaign speech.

The transformation extended beyond Trump's own communication to include changes in how political news was covered and consumed. His presidency accelerated the fragmentation of American media into partisan information ecosystems, with different audiences receiving fundamentally different information about political events and developments.

"Trump showed that the traditional media's role as gatekeeper had been permanently weakened," observed media critic Jay Rosen. "Politicians could now reach audiences directly through social media platforms, making traditional journalism less central to political communication."

The media transformation also included changes in journalistic practices, as news organizations struggled to cover a president who routinely made false statements and attacked their credibility. Trump's adversarial relationship with mainstream media created new challenges for political journalism that persisted long after his presidency.

Trump's breakthrough represented more than just a successful insurgent campaign—it reflected and accelerated a fundamental realignment of American electoral politics along lines of education, geography, and cultural identity rather than traditional economic divisions. His coalition brought together working-class voters of all races around themes of nationalism and cultural traditionalism.

The realignment was most evident in Trump's ability to attract white working-class voters who had previously supported Democratic candidates, while losing college-educated suburban voters who had historically voted Republican. This trade-off fundamentally altered the electoral map and the strategic calculations of both major political parties.

"Trump's 2016 victory represented the end of the New Deal coalition and the beginning of something entirely new," observed political analyst Sean Trende. "The old divisions between business Republicans and labor Democrats had been replaced by new divisions between cosmopolitan and nationalist worldviews."

The electoral realignment also had profound implications for American political geography, as Trump's coalition was concentrated in rural areas and smaller cities while his opponents' strength was concentrated in major metropolitan areas. This geographic polarization created new challenges for American democracy and governance.

Perhaps the most significant aspect of Trump's breakthrough was its challenge to the norms and institutions that had governed American politics for decades. His campaign and presidency tested the resilience of democratic institutions in ways that had not been attempted since the founding of the modern political system.

Trump's challenge to institutional norms was evident from his campaign announcement through his presidency and beyond. His refusal to release tax returns, his attacks on judicial decisions, his criticism of election procedures, and his questioning of intelligence agencies represented departures from practices that had been considered essential to democratic governance.

"Trump's entire political career was based on challenging the assumption that political leaders should respect institutional constraints," observed constitutional scholar Norm Ornstein. "His breakthrough showed that American voters were willing to support candidates who promised to break institutional rules they saw as ineffective or corrupt."

The institutional challenge posed by Trump's breakthrough raised fundamental questions about the stability and sustainability of American democratic institutions. His success demonstrated that these institutions depended more heavily on voluntary compliance and cultural norms than on legal requirements or constitutional provisions.

Trump's 2016 breakthrough had implications that extended far beyond American politics to influence political movements and electoral outcomes around the world. His success inspired populist and nationalist politicians in other countries who adopted similar rhetorical strategies and policy positions.

The global impact was particularly evident in the rise of Trump-like figures in other democracies who combined economic nationalism, cultural traditionalism, and anti-establishment rhetoric to build political coalitions. Trump's breakthrough provided a template for populist success that was adapted to different national contexts and political systems.

"Trump's victory sent shockwaves through the international political system," observed foreign policy analyst Ian Bremmer. "It showed that the liberal international order could be challenged from within by democratically elected leaders who rejected its fundamental premises."

The global influence of Trump's breakthrough also included changes in international relationships and institutions, as other world leaders were forced to adapt to an American president who questioned long-standing alliances and agreements. The 2016 election marked a turning point in America's role in global affairs that persisted beyond Trump's individual presidency.

Donald Trump's 2016 breakthrough stands as the most improbable and consequential political success story in modern American history. His transformation from reality television celebrity to President of the United States defied every conventional wisdom about American politics and demonstrated that under the right circumstances, the most unlikely candidates could achieve the most extraordinary victories.

Trump's success proved that political authenticity, media mastery, and anti-establishment appeal could overcome any disadvantage in experience, organization, or traditional political assets. His campaign showed that American voters were willing to support candidates who violated political norms if they believed those candidates would represent their interests more effectively than conventional politicians.

Yet Trump's breakthrough also revealed the fragility of democratic institutions and the potential for political polarization to undermine the shared values and common purposes that democratic societies require. His success created new possibilities for American politics while also creating new dangers for American democracy.

The real estate mogul from New York had accomplished something that political scientists had considered impossible: he had converted celebrity status and media manipulation into the ultimate political prize. His tidal wave had not just captured the presidency—it had fundamentally altered the landscape of American politics in ways that would influence elections and governance for generations to come.

Donald Trump had proven that in American politics, there were no impossible dreams for those who understood how to harness the forces of change, discontent, and hope that always exist beneath the surface of democratic societies. His breakthrough would inspire countless imitators while serving as a permanent reminder that in a democracy, the people retain the ultimate power to overturn any political establishment that fails to serve their needs and represent their values.

“The graceful nature of Buttigieg’s withdrawal enhanced his reputation within the Democratic Party and positioned him for future political opportunities at the national level.”

15

BUTTIGIEG BOOMLET (2020)

The text message that arrived on Mike Schmuhl's phone at 11:43 PM on February 3, 2020, contained just four words, but they represented the culmination of the most improbable political journey in modern Democratic primary history. "We're going to win," wrote Pete Buttigieg from his hotel room in Des Moines, where the 38-year-old former mayor of South Bend, Indiana, was monitoring returns from the Iowa Democratic caucuses with the quiet confidence of someone who had spent two years preparing for exactly this moment.

Hours earlier, few political observers would have believed such a message was possible. Buttigieg had entered the 2020 presidential race as the ultimate long-shot candidate: a small-city mayor with no national political experience, no significant fundraising network, and a resume that seemed laughably inadequate for the world's most powerful office. The Democratic field was dominated by senators, governors, and a former vice president who possessed every conceivable advantage in name recognition, organizational strength, and political credibility.

Yet as the chaotic Iowa results slowly emerged over the following days—plagued by technical failures that would overshadow the political story—it became clear that Buttigieg had indeed achieved something extraordinary. He had won the most delegates in Iowa, narrowly edging out Bernie Sanders in a victory that transformed him overnight from a curiosity into a genuine contender for the Democratic nomination.

"Nobody saw this coming," admitted David Axelrod, Barack Obama's former chief strategist, as he watched Buttigieg's victory speech on television. "A 38-year-old mayor from Indiana just beat senators and governors who have been preparing for this moment their entire careers. This is either the beginning of something remarkable or the political story of the year."

It would prove to be both. Buttigieg's breakthrough represented one of the most dramatic examples of how political momentum could elevate unknown candidates to national prominence in the modern media age. But it would also demonstrate the harsh realities that constrain even the most talented breakthrough candidates when they encounter the diverse coalitions and complex demographics that determine Democratic nominations.

Pete Buttigieg's decision to seek the presidency seemed to defy every rule of modern political ambition. At 37, when he announced his exploratory committee in January 2019, he was young enough to be the son of most of his competitors. His highest elected office was mayor of a city with 100,000 residents, smaller than most congressional districts and a fraction of the size of the states that senators and governors were accustomed to governing.

Yet Buttigieg possessed a combination of intellectual gifts and personal qualities that had distinguished him throughout his remarkable academic and professional career. A Rhodes Scholar and Harvard graduate, he had served as a Navy intelligence officer in Afghanistan before returning to South Bend to become the youngest mayor of a U.S. city with more than 100,000 residents. His fluency in seven languages, his thoughtful approach to policy issues, and his obvious intellectual curiosity suggested a depth of preparation that many more experienced politicians lacked.

"Pete understood that in the modern Democratic Party, intellectual credibility and policy sophistication could substitute for traditional political experience," observed Lis Smith, who served as his communications advisor. "He might not have been a senator, but he could talk about any issue with the kind of knowledge and nuance that impressed voters who valued competence and thoughtfulness."

Buttigieg's personal story also provided compelling narrative elements that distinguished him from his competitors. As an openly gay candidate who had married his husband Chasten during his mayoral tenure, he represented generational and social change within the Democratic Party. His military service in Afghanistan gave him foreign policy credibility that few domestic politicians possessed. His midwestern background and small-city experience allowed him to speak authentically about the concerns of voters in the industrial heartland that Democrats needed to reclaim.

The challenge for Buttigieg was how to convert these personal and intellectual assets into the kind of political organization and media attention that could make him competitive against better-known opponents. His campaign would need to demonstrate that voters were ready to support a candidate based on potential rather than experience, and that the Democratic Party was prepared to take a remarkable risk on an untested leader.

Buttigieg's breakthrough began with a political message that was perfectly calibrated for the moment in Democratic politics: the promise of generational change coupled with a return to the pragmatic liberalism that had characterized the party's most successful leaders. His campaign theme of representing "a new generation of leadership" provided a subtle but effective critique of both the septuagenarian frontrunners in the Democratic field and the divisive politics that had characterized the Trump era.

"Pete's genius was understanding that Democratic voters wanted change, but they also wanted competence and stability," explained his senior advisor Mike Schmuhl. "He could represent the future without seeming risky, and he could criticize the past without seeming disrespectful to the party's achievements."

The generational message was particularly effective because it allowed Buttigieg to position himself as the candidate of both continuity and change. He could embrace the policy legacy of Barack Obama while arguing that new leadership was needed to face contemporary challenges. He could criticize the failures of Washington politics while demonstrating his own mastery of policy details and political communication.

Buttigieg's approach to contentious issues within the Democratic Party also reflected his strategic understanding of how to appeal to different constituencies simultaneously. On healthcare, he supported expanding coverage while avoiding the divisive Medicare for All debate that separated progressive and moderate Democrats. On climate change, he emphasized technological innovation and economic opportunity rather than economic sacrifice. On foreign policy, he combined criticism of military interventions with support for strong international engagement.

The message resonated particularly strongly with college-educated professionals who formed an increasingly important part of the Democratic coalition. These voters appreciated Buttigieg's intellectual approach to policy questions and his ability to articulate complex positions with clarity and nuance. His calm, professorial demeanor provided a stark contrast to the emotional intensity that characterized much of contemporary political discourse.

Buttigieg's breakthrough required a strategic gamble that echoed successful insurgent campaigns from previous election cycles: he would invest disproportionate resources in Iowa, betting that a strong performance there could generate the momentum and credibility needed to compete in subsequent contests. The decision was risky because failure in Iowa would likely end his campaign before it truly began, but success could transform him from an unknown into a legitimate contender.

The Iowa strategy played to Buttigieg's strengths as a retail politician who excelled in the kind of intimate, personal campaigning that the state's political culture rewarded. His ability to connect with voters in small groups, his mastery of policy details, and his obvious sincerity all translated effectively to Iowa's town halls, coffee shops, and living room gatherings.

"Iowa was perfect for Pete because it allowed him to demonstrate his knowledge and authenticity in settings where those qualities really mattered," observed Jeff Link, a veteran Iowa Democratic strategist who worked with the campaign. "He could have hour-long conversations about agricultural policy with farmers, discuss manufacturing with union workers, and talk about education with teachers. That kind of deep engagement is what Iowa voters expect and appreciate."

Buttigieg's Iowa organization was built around the community organizing principles that successful caucus campaigns require: identifying potential supporters, building personal relationships, and ensuring that committed caucus-goers actually participated in the complex delegate selection process. His campaign hired experienced Iowa operatives who understood the state's unique political dynamics and invested in the kind of grassroots organizing that could maximize turnout among his supporters.

The campaign's approach to Iowa also reflected Buttigieg's understanding of how media coverage worked in the modern political environment. His strong debate performances and thoughtful policy speeches generated positive coverage that improved his name recognition and credibility with Iowa voters. His campaign's sophisticated digital operation allowed him to reach younger voters who might not attend traditional political events but who could be mobilized through social media and online organizing.

Buttigieg's emergence as a serious contender began with his performances in the Democratic primary debates, where his combination of policy knowledge, communication skills, and personal authenticity distinguished him from more experienced but less compelling competitors. His breakout moment came during the first debate in June 2019, when his thoughtful responses to questions about foreign policy and social issues demonstrated that he belonged on the same stage as senators and governors.

"The debates were crucial for Pete because they gave him a national platform to show voters what he could do," recalled debate prep coordinator Sean Savett. "He wasn't well-known enough to command attention on his own, but when he was on stage with other candidates, his intelligence and communication skills really stood out."

Buttigieg's debate performances were particularly effective because they showcased his ability to discuss controversial topics with nuance and sophistication rather than simple talking points. His responses to questions about policing and racial justice demonstrated his willingness to acknowledge complexity and uncertainty rather than offering easy answers to difficult problems. His discussions of foreign policy reflected his military experience and his understanding of international relations.

The debates also revealed Buttigieg's strategic approach to primary politics. Rather than attacking his opponents directly, he typically focused on presenting his own vision and qualifications, allowing voters to make their own comparisons. When he did engage in confrontations, they were usually over policy differences rather than personal attacks, reinforcing his image as a serious candidate focused on substantive issues.

Media coverage of Buttigieg's debate performances generated exactly the kind of momentum that breakthrough campaigns require. Political reporters began writing profiles of the "mayor from Indiana" who was impressing audiences with his thoughtfulness and preparation. Cable news programs featured discussions of whether Democratic voters were ready to support such a young and inexperienced candidate for president.

Buttigieg's debate performances triggered a remarkable surge in small-dollar fundraising that demonstrated the genuine enthusiasm his candidacy was generating among Democratic donors. His second-quarter fundraising total of $24.8 million exceeded the totals raised by several better-known senators and governors, proving that his appeal extended beyond media coverage to include actual financial support from voters.

The fundraising success was particularly impressive because it came primarily from small-dollar donors who were responding to Buttigieg's message and persona rather than being cultivated through traditional political networks. His campaign's emphasis on online fundraising and digital outreach allowed him to tap into networks of Democratic donors who had not been reached by other campaigns.

"The fundraising numbers showed that Pete's support was real and growing," acknowledged his finance director, Ryan Montoya. "We weren't just getting good coverage—we were building a base of committed supporters who were willing to invest in his candidacy with their own money."

The financial resources also allowed Buttigieg's campaign to expand its operations beyond Iowa to include early organizing in New Hampshire, Nevada, and South Carolina. While he maintained his strategic focus on Iowa, the additional resources provided insurance against the possibility that his Iowa gamble might not pay off and created opportunities for sustained momentum if his breakthrough succeeded.

Buttigieg's fundraising success also forced other campaigns and political observers to take his candidacy more seriously. Candidates who had initially dismissed him as a novelty began treating him as a legitimate competitor, while political reporters started covering his campaign with the attention typically reserved for frontrunners.

When Iowa Democrats gathered for their caucuses on February 3, 2020, Buttigieg's two-year investment in the state paid off with a narrow but decisive victory that exceeded even his campaign's optimistic projections. His 26.2 percent of state delegate equivalents, just ahead of Bernie Sanders' 26.0 percent, represented a stunning upset that transformed the entire Democratic primary race.

The Iowa victory was particularly impressive because it demonstrated Buttigieg's ability to build a broad coalition within the Democratic Party. His support came not just from college-educated professionals who had been drawn to his intellectual approach, but also from rural Democrats, older voters, and moderate Republicans who appreciated his pragmatic positions and unifying message.

"Iowa showed that Pete could appeal to Democrats across demographic and geographic lines," observed Tom Henderson, chairman of the Polk County Democrats. "He won in Des Moines, and he won in small rural counties. He attracted young professionals and retired farmers. That kind of broad appeal is exactly what you need to win in Iowa."

The victory also validated Buttigieg's strategic decision to focus intensively on Iowa rather than spreading his resources across multiple early states. His superior organization and personal relationships with Iowa voters had overcome the name recognition and media advantages possessed by his better-known competitors.

The Iowa breakthrough generated exactly the kind of national media coverage that can transform unknown candidates into household names overnight. Television networks devoted extensive coverage to Buttigieg's upset victory, with reporters analyzing how a small-city mayor had managed to defeat senators and governors with decades of political experience.

Buttigieg's Iowa victory created momentum that carried him to a strong second-place finish in New Hampshire on February 11, 2020, where his 24.4 percent showing behind Bernie Sanders (25.7 percent) demonstrated that his appeal could extend beyond Iowa's unique political culture to include voters in other early primary states.

The New Hampshire result was particularly significant because it occurred in a state with a very different political culture from Iowa. Where Iowa Democrats were primarily rural and moderate, New Hampshire Democrats included large numbers of suburban professionals and liberal activists who might have been expected to support different candidates. Buttigieg's ability to compete effectively in both states suggested that his breakthrough might be sustainable.

"New Hampshire proved that Iowa wasn't a fluke," reflected New Hampshire Democratic strategist Jim Demers. "Pete showed that he could adapt his message to different audiences while maintaining his core appeal as a thoughtful, unifying candidate."

The New Hampshire campaign also showcased Buttigieg's evolution as a national political figure. His town halls and campaign events drew overflow crowds, demonstrating the genuine enthusiasm his candidacy was generating among Democratic voters. His media interviews revealed increasing confidence and sophistication in discussing national issues beyond his previous experience as a small-city mayor.

The combination of Iowa and New Hampshire results established Buttigieg as one of the top three candidates in the Democratic field, alongside Sanders and Joe Biden. His fundraising increased dramatically following his early state successes, allowing his campaign to expand operations and compete more effectively in upcoming primary contests.

Despite his impressive early state successes, Buttigieg's breakthrough began to encounter significant limitations when the primary calendar moved to more diverse states, where his appeal among minority voters proved to be much weaker than his support among white Democrats. His poor performance in Nevada and South Carolina revealed the narrow demographic base of his coalition and raised questions about his viability in a party where minority voters formed crucial constituencies.

The diversity challenge was evident in Buttigieg's third-place finish in Nevada on February 22, where he won just 14.3 percent of the vote and struggled particularly with Latino voters who formed a large part of the state's Democratic electorate. His campaign's limited investment in Spanish-language outreach and his lack of relationships with Latino political leaders contributed to his poor showing in a state that should have been competitive for a candidate with his early momentum.

"Nevada showed that Pete's coalition was narrower than we had hoped," acknowledged a senior campaign adviser. "He was incredibly strong with college-educated white voters, but we hadn't figured out how to expand his appeal to the diverse communities that are essential for winning Democratic primaries."

The challenge became even more apparent in South Carolina on February 29, where Buttigieg's fourth-place finish with just 8.2 percent of the vote demonstrated his limited appeal among African American voters who formed a majority of the state's Democratic primary electorate. Despite months of campaigning and significant resource investments, his campaign had failed to build meaningful relationships with Black political leaders or develop messages that resonated with African American voters.

The diversity challenge reflected broader questions about Buttigieg's experience and background that had not been apparent during his early successes in predominantly white states. His tenure as mayor of South Bend had included controversial incidents involving police and the African American community that had received limited attention during his Iowa and New Hampshire campaigns but became major issues when his candidacy faced scrutiny from minority voters and political leaders.

Buttigieg's breakthrough momentum effectively ended on Super Tuesday, March 3, 2020, when his campaign's organizational and demographic limitations became apparent across multiple large and diverse primary states. His inability to compete effectively beyond his narrow base of support forced him to confront the reality that his remarkable early success could not be sustained across the broader Democratic primary electorate.

The Super Tuesday results were devastating for Buttigieg's campaign. Despite his early state successes and the momentum they had generated, he won no states and finished fourth or worse in most contests. His best performance was a third-place finish in Minnesota with 12.2 percent, while he struggled to reach double digits in most other states.

"Super Tuesday showed that Pete's early success had been built on a foundation that was too narrow to sustain a national campaign," observed Democratic strategist James Carville. "He had created genuine excitement among certain types of Democratic voters, but he hadn't figured out how to expand his appeal to the full range of constituencies needed to win the nomination."

The poor Super Tuesday results also revealed the organizational challenges that had constrained Buttigieg's campaign despite its impressive fundraising and early momentum. His campaign lacked the infrastructure needed to compete effectively in multiple large states simultaneously, while his message and coalition-building efforts had not adapted successfully to the diverse political environments that characterized different regions of the country.

On March 1, 2020, just two days before Super Tuesday, Buttigieg made the difficult decision to suspend his presidential campaign, acknowledging that his path to the Democratic nomination had become mathematically impossible despite his remarkable achievements over the previous year. His withdrawal speech captured both the disappointment of ending a breakthrough campaign and his understanding of the broader political moment facing the Democratic Party.

"We must recognize that at this point in the race, the best way to keep faith with those goals and those values is to step aside and help bring our party and our country together," Buttigieg said in his withdrawal speech in South Bend. "So tonight, I am making the difficult decision to suspend my campaign for the presidency."

The withdrawal was strategically timed to maximize its impact on the Super Tuesday contests, where Buttigieg's endorsement of Joe Biden would help consolidate moderate Democratic support around the former vice president's candidacy. The decision demonstrated Buttigieg's understanding of his role in the broader Democratic coalition and his willingness to prioritize party unity over personal ambition.

The graceful nature of Buttigieg's withdrawal enhanced his reputation within the Democratic Party and positioned him for future political opportunities at the national level. His decision to endorse Biden immediately and campaign actively for the eventual nominee reinforced his image as a team player who understood the importance of defeating Donald Trump over advancing his own political career.

Despite his ultimate failure to secure the Democratic nomination, Buttigieg's 2020 breakthrough represented several historic achievements that will influence American politics for years to come. He became the first openly gay candidate to win delegates in a major party's presidential primary, demonstrating that sexual orientation was no longer an insurmountable barrier to national political success.

Buttigieg's breakthrough also proved that political talent and intellectual capability could still elevate unknown candidates to national prominence in an era increasingly dominated by celebrity and name recognition. His transformation from small-city mayor to serious presidential contender showed that the American political system remained open to fresh faces and new ideas when they were presented with sufficient skill and strategic sophistication.

"Pete's campaign showed that the barriers to presidential politics were lower than most people realized," observed political scientist David Hopkins. "If a 38-year-old mayor from Indiana could become a serious contender for president, it meant that talented politicians didn't have to spend decades climbing traditional career ladders to compete at the highest levels."

The campaign also demonstrated the continuing importance of early primary states in determining presidential nominations. Buttigieg's strategic focus on Iowa and New Hampshire had allowed him to overcome enormous disadvantages in name recognition and institutional support, at least temporarily, proving that the current primary system still provided opportunities for breakthrough candidates.

Buttigieg's impressive primary campaign and his subsequent support for Joe Biden's candidacy were rewarded with his nomination as Secretary of Transportation in the Biden administration, making him the first openly gay person to serve in a presidential cabinet. The appointment validated his policy expertise and political skills while providing him with executive branch experience that could prove valuable in future political endeavors.

The cabinet position also allowed Buttigieg to maintain his national political profile and continue building relationships with Democratic leaders and voters across the country. His performance as Transportation Secretary, particularly his handling of infrastructure initiatives and his communication of administration policies, reinforced his reputation as a thoughtful and competent public servant.

"The cabinet position was perfect for Pete because it allowed him to gain executive experience while staying visible on the national political scene," observed Democratic strategist Jennifer Palmieri. "He's still young enough that this could be just the beginning of a very significant political career."

Buttigieg's 2020 breakthrough established him as one of the most promising figures in the Democratic Party's next generation of leaders, with political assets that could serve him well in future campaigns for governor, senator, or president. His demonstrated ability to attract national attention and build diverse coalitions, combined with his policy expertise and communication skills, positioned him as a likely candidate for higher office in the coming decades.

The campaign also provided valuable lessons about the changing nature of Democratic primary politics and the continuing importance of early state performance in building national political momentum. Buttigieg's success in Iowa and New Hampshire showed that breakthrough moments remained possible for candidates who understood how to combine authentic messaging with strategic discipline and superior organization.

Perhaps most importantly, Buttigieg's breakthrough demonstrated that American politics remained capable of producing genuine surprises and that political talent could still triumph over traditional advantages in the right circumstances. His remarkable journey from small-city mayor to serious presidential contender reminded observers that in American democracy, almost anything remained possible for candidates who possessed the vision, skills, and determination to pursue their highest ambitions.

Pete Buttigieg's 2020 campaign stands as one of the most remarkable breakthrough stories in modern American political history, demonstrating how quickly unknown candidates could rise to national prominence when they possessed the right combination of talent, strategy, and timing. His Iowa victory and early primary success proved that the political system remained open to fresh faces and new ideas, even in an era increasingly dominated by celebrity and name recognition.

Yet Buttigieg's ultimate inability to sustain his breakthrough beyond predominantly white early primary states also revealed the persistent challenges facing candidates whose appeal is concentrated among narrow demographic constituencies. His experience illustrated the difference between creating exciting moments and building the broad coalitions necessary for sustained political success.

The tragedy of Buttigieg's breakthrough was not that he lost—most insurgent candidates do—but that his obvious talents for political communication and coalition-building were not yet matched by the experience and relationships needed to appeal to the full diversity of the Democratic coalition. His campaign had shown that he could inspire certain types of Democratic voters, but it had not yet solved the puzzle of how to expand that inspiration to include all the communities that modern Democratic candidates must mobilize.

The young mayor from South Bend had accomplished something extraordinary: he had converted intellectual capability and political authenticity into serious consideration for the world's most powerful office. His boomlet had burned brightly across the Democratic primary landscape, illuminating new possibilities for American politics while also revealing the enduring challenges that face breakthrough candidates in a diverse democracy.

Pete Buttigieg had proven that in American politics, meteoric rises remained possible for those who understood how to combine personal authenticity with strategic sophistication. His shooting star had not reached the presidency, but it had established him as a major figure in Democratic politics and demonstrated that the next generation of American leaders was ready to step forward when the moment was right.

"Nikki Haley's breakthrough stands as one of the most impressive second-place finishes in modern Republican primary history."

16

HALEY FLASH (2024)

The debate hall at the University of Alabama was electric with tension as Nikki Haley stepped to her podium on December 6, 2023, for what many observers considered the make-or-break moment of her presidential campaign. For months, the former South Carolina governor and UN Ambassador had been trapped in the second tier of Republican candidates, overshadowed by Donald Trump's dominant polling lead and Ron DeSantis's early positioning as the principal alternative to the former president.

But as Haley looked across the stage at her competitors—DeSantis, Vivek Ramaswamy, and Chris Christie—she sensed an opportunity that had been building throughout the primary campaign. Republican voters were growing weary of Trump's legal troubles and backward-looking grievances, yet they remained skeptical of DeSantis's increasingly forced attempts to out-Trump Trump. The party seemed ready for someone who could articulate conservative principles without the personal baggage and divisive rhetoric that had defined Republican politics since 2016.

"I'm not running to be Trump 2.0," Haley declared during her closing statement, looking directly into the camera rather than at her opponents. "I'm running to be the president America needs for the next generation. We need to stop looking backward and start looking forward. We need to win elections again, not just make excuses for why we lost them."

The line drew sustained applause from the audience and generated exactly the kind of viral moment that modern campaigns require to break through media clutter and capture voter attention. Within hours, clips of Haley's performance were circulating on social media, cable news programs were analyzing her "breakthrough moment," and political reporters were writing stories about the "Haley surge" that seemed to be building across early primary states.

Less than two months later, that surge would peak with Haley's surprisingly strong second-place finish in New Hampshire, where her 43.2 percent showing against Trump's 54.3 percent would demonstrate that Republican voters were indeed ready to consider alternatives to the former president—even if they weren't quite ready to choose them over the man who had dominated their party for nearly a decade.

Nikki Haley's path to the 2024 Republican presidential nomination represented one of the most strategically sophisticated campaigns in modern primary politics, combining careful positioning with tactical patience in ways that distinguished her from the more impulsive approaches of her competitors. Unlike candidates who had built their careers around opposition to Trump or excessive loyalty to him, Haley had navigated the complex dynamics of Trump-era Republican politics with remarkable skill, maintaining her conservative credentials while preserving her independence.

Haley's political biography provided exactly the kind of profile that Republican strategists believed their party needed to compete effectively in post-Trump politics. As the daughter of Indian immigrants who had become the first woman and first minority to serve as governor of South Carolina, she embodied the demographic diversity that party leaders knew was essential for long-term electoral success. Her tenure as UN Ambassador had given her foreign policy credentials that few of her competitors possessed, while her conservative record as governor established her bona fides with the Republican base.

"Nikki represented the future of the Republican Party that a lot of people wanted to see," observed Republican strategist Mike DuHaime. "She had the resume, the demographic profile, and the political skills to appeal to suburban voters who had left the party during the Trump years while maintaining credibility with conservative activists."

Haley's decision to seek the presidency reflected her belief that the Republican Party was ready to move beyond Trump's divisive leadership style while maintaining its conservative policy commitments. Her campaign message of "strong and proud America" emphasized traditional conservative themes of fiscal responsibility, strong national defense, and limited government while avoiding the cultural grievances and personal attacks that had characterized Trump's approach to politics.

The challenge for Haley was how to differentiate herself from Trump without alienating his supporters, while simultaneously positioning herself as a more electable alternative without seeming disloyal to the party's dominant figure. Her campaign would need to thread the needle between appealing to Trump-skeptical Republicans and maintaining credibility with the former president's passionate base of support.

Haley's breakthrough began with a strategic approach to the Republican primary that was notable for its discipline and precision. While other candidates either embraced Trump completely or rejected him entirely, Haley adopted a more nuanced position that acknowledged his policy achievements while criticizing his personal behavior and electability problems.

"Nikki's strategy was surgical," explained her senior adviser Betsy Ankney. "She wasn't going to attack Trump personally or question his conservative credentials, but she was going to make the case that the party needed to move forward with new leadership that could actually win elections."

This positioning allowed Haley to appeal to different constituencies within the Republican coalition simultaneously. Republican voters who remained loyal to Trump could appreciate her defense of his policy record, while those who had grown weary of his controversies could see her as a viable alternative who shared their conservative values without the associated political baggage.

Haley's approach was particularly evident in her handling of Trump's legal troubles, which dominated Republican primary coverage throughout 2023. Rather than defending Trump's behavior or attacking the justice system, she expressed sympathy for his legal difficulties while arguing that Republicans needed a nominee who could focus on defeating Democrats rather than fighting legal battles.

"I think President Trump was the right president at the right time," Haley said in a typical formulation. "But I think it's time for a new generation of leadership." The message allowed her to maintain respect for Trump's presidency while making the case for change without seeming bitter or disloyal.

Haley's breakthrough was powered by a series of increasingly impressive debate performances that showcased her policy knowledge, communication skills, and ability to project strength without resorting to the personal attacks that characterized many of her competitors' approaches. Her performances in the Republican primary debates became the foundation for her campaign's momentum and the primary vehicle for introducing her to Republican voters who were unfamiliar with her background.

The August 23, 2023, debate in Milwaukee marked the beginning of Haley's ascent, as she distinguished herself from a crowded field of candidates through crisp answers and strategic confrontations with her rivals. Her exchange with Vivek Ramaswamy, where she criticized his lack of foreign policy experience, demonstrated her ability to go on the offensive without appearing mean-spirited or unpresidential.

"Every time I hear you, I feel a little bit dumber for what you say," Haley told Ramaswamy during one particularly effective exchange, drawing laughter from the audience and generating viral social media coverage that expanded her reach beyond traditional political audiences.

"The debates were crucial for Nikki because they allowed her to show Republican voters what she could do under pressure," recalled debate prep coordinator Rob Burgess. "She could handle policy questions, she could defend her record, and she could take on opponents without looking petty or harsh. That combination is exactly what many Republicans were looking for."

Haley's debate performances were particularly effective because they demonstrated her evolution as a national political figure. The candidate who had sometimes appeared stiff or overly programmed in earlier appearances became more natural and confident as the debate season progressed, showing an ability to connect with audiences while maintaining her command of policy details.

Each subsequent debate reinforced Haley's image as the most presidential candidate in the field besides Trump, who was notably absent from most of these forums. Her ability to discuss complex international issues with authority, combined with her crisp delivery and apparent comfort under pressure, suggested that she possessed the qualifications necessary for the presidency in ways that some of her competitors did not.

Despite her strong debate performances, Haley made a strategic decision that would ultimately limit her breakthrough potential: she chose not to invest heavily in Iowa, instead focusing her resources on New Hampshire and South Carolina, where she believed her message would resonate more effectively with Republican primary voters.

The Iowa decision reflected Haley's understanding of her own political strengths and weaknesses. Iowa's Republican caucus electorate was heavily evangelical and populist, constituencies that had historically been more receptive to candidates like Trump, Ted Cruz, and Ron DeSantis. Haley's more establishment-oriented conservative message and her foreign policy focus were less likely to resonate with Iowa Republicans who prioritized cultural issues and economic nationalism.

"We made a conscious decision to focus on states where Nikki's message and background would be most effective," acknowledged campaign manager Ankney. "Iowa was always going to be challenging for us because of the evangelical and populist nature of the electorate. We thought we could be more competitive in New Hampshire and South Carolina."

The Iowa strategy allowed Haley to concentrate her limited resources on states where she had natural advantages. New Hampshire's more secular and educated Republican electorate was likely to appreciate her policy expertise and measured approach to politics. South Carolina, where she had served as governor, provided her with name recognition and organizational advantages that could compensate for her relatively modest fundraising compared to Trump and DeSantis.

However, the decision to largely bypass Iowa also meant that Haley would miss an opportunity to demonstrate her electoral viability in the state that had historically been crucial for establishing momentum in Republican primary campaigns. Her third-place finish in Iowa with just 19.1 percent of the vote reinforced perceptions that her appeal was limited to certain types of Republican voters rather than representing broad-based support within the party.

Haley's most significant breakthrough moment came in New Hampshire, where her intensive campaigning and strategic positioning culminated in a strong second-place finish that exceeded expectations and demonstrated her potential as a viable alternative to Trump. Her 43.2 percent showing against

Trump's 54.3 percent represented the strongest performance by any Trump challenger in the 2024 primary season.

The New Hampshire campaign showcased all of Haley's strengths as a candidate and highlighted the appeal of her message to the educated, suburban Republicans who had become increasingly important in post-Trump electoral politics. Her town halls and campaign events drew overflow crowds, demonstrating genuine enthusiasm for her candidacy among voters who were looking for conservative leadership without Trump's divisive rhetoric.

"New Hampshire was where everything came together for Nikki," reflected New Hampshire state director Juliana Bergeron. "Her debate performances had introduced her to voters, her policy positions resonated with the state's electorate, and her campaign organization was finally operating at the level she needed to compete with Trump's operation."

Haley's New Hampshire campaign also benefited from the strategic decisions of her opponents. DeSantis had largely written off the state to focus on Iowa and South Carolina, while other Trump alternatives like Chris Christie withdrew from the race. These developments allowed Haley to consolidate anti-Trump support in a way that had not been possible in previous contests.

The New Hampshire result generated exactly the kind of momentum that breakthrough candidates require. Media coverage of her strong showing portrayed her as the last credible alternative to Trump, while her fundraising increased dramatically in the days following the primary. Her campaign attracted endorsements from Republican donors and elected officials who had been waiting to see evidence of her viability before committing their support.

More importantly, the New Hampshire result demonstrated that Republican voters were indeed willing to consider alternatives to Trump when presented with a candidate who combined conservative credentials with electability arguments. Exit polls showed that Haley had performed particularly well among Republican voters who were concerned about Trump's legal troubles and his ability to defeat Joe Biden in a general election.

Haley's breakthrough faced its ultimate test in South Carolina, her home state and the place where her political career had begun. The

February 24 primary represented her best opportunity to prove that her New Hampshire performance had been more than a regional anomaly and that she could build the kind of broad-based support necessary to challenge Trump's dominance within the Republican Party.

The South Carolina campaign revealed both Haley's potential and her limitations as a breakthrough candidate. Her advantages as a former governor were evident in her detailed knowledge of state issues and her relationships with local political leaders. Her campaign organization was superior to those of her competitors, and her fundraising allowed her to compete effectively in paid advertising and voter outreach efforts.

Yet the South Carolina results also exposed the narrow demographic base of Haley's support within the Republican Party. Despite her advantages as a native daughter and former governor, she won just 39.5 percent of the vote to Trump's 60.0 percent, a margin that demonstrated the continuing strength of Trump's hold on Republican voters even in states where his opponents had natural advantages.

"South Carolina showed that Nikki's ceiling within the Republican Party was lower than we had hoped," acknowledged a senior campaign adviser. "She could compete with Trump among certain types of Republican voters—suburban professionals, college graduates, women—but she couldn't expand her appeal to the working-class and evangelical voters who formed the core of Trump's support."

The South Carolina defeat was particularly disappointing because it occurred despite favorable circumstances for Haley's candidacy. The primary was held in her home state, where she had high name recognition and positive approval ratings. The field had been winnowed to essentially a two-person race between her and Trump, eliminating the vote-splitting that had benefited Trump in previous contests. Her campaign had months to organize and had superior financial resources compared to most primary challenges.

On March 5, 2024, Haley announced the suspension of her presidential campaign, acknowledging that her path to the Republican nomination had become mathematically impossible despite her strong performances in New Hampshire and other early states. Her withdrawal speech captured both the achievement of her breakthrough campaign and her understanding of the broader challenges facing the Republican Party.

“The time has now come to suspend my campaign,” Haley said in remarks outside her campaign headquarters in Charleston. “I said I wanted Americans to have their voices heard. I have done that. I have no regrets.”

The withdrawal was timed to occur before Super Tuesday, allowing Haley to exit the race with dignity rather than suffering additional defeats that might damage her future political prospects. Her decision not to immediately endorse Trump demonstrated her continued independence and maintained her credibility with Republican voters who shared her concerns about the former president’s electability and behavior.

Haley’s campaign had lasted longer than those of most Trump challengers and had achieved more success than many observers had predicted when she entered the race. Her ability to compete effectively in multiple states and to maintain her campaign through numerous primary contests demonstrated both her political skills and the genuine enthusiasm her candidacy had generated among certain segments of the Republican electorate.

Despite her ultimate failure to secure the Republican nomination, Haley’s 2024 breakthrough represented several significant achievements that will influence Republican politics and American political development for years to come. She became the most successful woman candidate in Republican primary history, winning more votes and delegates than any previous female Republican presidential contender.

Haley’s campaign also demonstrated that there remained a significant appetite within the Republican Party for conservative leadership that was not defined by loyalty to Trump or opposition to him. Her ability to win over 40 percent of Republican primary voters in multiple states showed that the party contained substantial constituencies who were ready for different approaches to conservative politics.

“Nikki proved that the Republican Party was more diverse in its thinking than many people realized,” observed Republican strategist Sarah Longwell. “There were millions of Republican voters who wanted conservative policies without Trump’s baggage, and she showed that those voters could be mobilized behind the right candidate with the right message.”

The campaign also established Haley as one of the most prominent figures in post-Trump Republican politics, positioning her as a likely leader in the party’s efforts to rebuild and expand its electoral coalition.

Her strong performances in suburban areas and among college-educated voters pointed toward the demographic groups that Republicans would need to reclaim in order to remain competitive in national elections.

Haley's breakthrough provided important insights into the changing dynamics of Republican primary politics and the challenges facing candidates who attempt to build coalitions that extend beyond Trump's base of support. Her success among certain demographic groups—suburban women, college graduates, younger Republicans—revealed constituencies within the party that were receptive to different approaches to conservative politics.

The campaign also demonstrated the continuing importance of debate performances and media coverage in shaping primary elections. Haley's rise in the polls correlated directly with her strong debate showings, while her ability to generate positive coverage helped her overcome significant disadvantages in fundraising and organization compared to Trump's campaign.

"Nikki's campaign showed that debates still matter in presidential politics," observed Republican debate strategist Brett O'Donnell. "Her performances allowed her to introduce herself to Republican voters and demonstrate her qualifications in ways that paid advertising or campaign events couldn't match. That's a lesson that future candidates should remember."

However, Haley's ultimate inability to expand her coalition beyond educated, suburban Republicans also revealed the persistent challenges facing candidates who represent significant departures from their party's dominant coalitions. Her campaign demonstrated that breakthrough moments in modern primaries require not just strong performances in favorable states but the ability to appeal to the full range of constituencies that participate in party nominations.

Haley's 2024 breakthrough established her as one of the most likely candidates to lead the Republican Party in the post-Trump era, whenever that might arrive. Her demonstration of electoral strength, combined with her policy expertise and communication skills, positioned her as a probable candidate for president, governor, or senator in future election cycles.

The campaign also provided valuable experience and visibility that could serve Haley well in subsequent political endeavors. Her ability to compete effectively on a national stage, raise significant amounts of money, and build organizations in multiple states demonstrated political capabilities that few Republicans possessed.

"Nikki's 2024 campaign was really about building for the future," reflected former Republican National Committee chairman Michael Steele. "She established herself as a major figure in Republican politics and positioned herself to be the leader when the party is ready to move beyond Trump. That could be 2028, or it could be earlier if circumstances change."

The breakthrough also influenced discussions within the Republican Party about its future direction and the qualities that successful candidates would need to possess in changing electoral environments. Haley's success among suburban voters and her ability to attract support from Democrats and independents in open primary states pointed toward strategic approaches that might be necessary for Republican electoral success.

Nikki Haley's 2024 breakthrough stands as one of the most impressive second-place finishes in modern Republican primary history, demonstrating how skilled candidates could build significant political movements even when competing against dominant frontrunners with overwhelming advantages in name recognition and organizational support.

Haley's campaign proved that breakthrough moments remained possible in contemporary Republican politics for candidates who could combine conservative credentials with electability arguments and superior communication skills. Her strong debate performances and New Hampshire showing demonstrated that Republican voters remained open to alternatives when presented with candidates who offered competence and optimism rather than grievance and division.

Yet Haley's ultimate inability to overcome Trump's hold on Republican voters also revealed the persistent constraints that face breakthrough candidates who represent significant departures from their party's prevailing orthodoxies. Her campaign had succeeded in attracting passionate support from certain constituencies within the Republican coalition, but it had not succeeded in building the kind of majority coalition that successful presidential campaigns require.

The tragedy of Haley's breakthrough was not that she lost—most challengers to dominant frontrunners do—but that her obvious qualifications for presidential leadership and her clear electoral advantages in a general election were insufficient to overcome the party loyalty and cultural attachments that bound Republican voters to Trump despite his legal troubles and electoral vulnerabilities.

The former governor and UN Ambassador had accomplished something remarkable: she had converted policy expertise and strategic positioning into serious consideration for the Republican presidential nomination despite starting the campaign with limited name recognition and modest organizational advantages. Her flash had illuminated possibilities for conservative politics that extended beyond Trump's divisive approach while demonstrating the enduring power of personal loyalty and cultural identity in contemporary partisan politics.

Nikki Haley had proven that in American politics, breakthrough candidates could still emerge from strategic patience combined with tactical excellence. Her shooting star had not captured the Republican nomination, but it had established her as a major figure in conservative politics and demonstrated that the party contained substantial constituencies ready for different approaches to conservative governance when the right moment and the right candidate converged.

The question for the future was whether Haley's flash represented a preview of Republican politics after Trump or simply another example of a talented candidate whose breakthrough came too early to be sustained. Only time would tell whether her impressive showing in 2024 had been the beginning of a new chapter in Republican politics or simply the brightest moment of a shooting star that had appeared before its season had truly arrived.

“Successful breakthrough candidates understood that winning presidential nominations required building governing coalitions, not just movement politics.”

CONCLUSION

On the evening of February 1, 2016, as results from the Iowa Republican caucuses slowly trickled in, a curious phenomenon was unfolding in campaign headquarters across Des Moines. In different rooms, surrounded by different advisers and addressing different audiences, three candidates were each claiming victory in their own way.

Donald Trump, despite finishing second to Ted Cruz, was already spinning his performance as better than expected for a political newcomer. Marco Rubio, having finished third with just 23 percent, was declaring his "three-two-one" showing a victory that established him as the establishment alternative to Cruz and Trump. And Cruz, the actual winner, was proclaiming his triumph as the beginning of a conservative revolution that would sweep him to the Republican nomination.

All three interpretations would prove partially correct and ultimately wrong. Trump's second-place finish in Iowa was indeed the beginning of an unprecedented political breakthrough that would carry him to the presidency. Rubio's strong third-place showing did establish him as a serious contender, but only briefly—his campaign would collapse after a disastrous debate performance just days before the New Hampshire primary. Cruz's Iowa victory did demonstrate his appeal to evangelical conservatives, but he would never again match that level of success as the primary calendar moved to more diverse states.

The Iowa results captured perfectly the central paradox that defines this book: the same primary system that creates opportunities for dramatic breakthrough moments also contains mechanisms that quickly expose the limitations of candidates who cannot expand their initial success into sustained political coalitions. Trump succeeded where Rubio and Cruz failed, not because he was a more traditional politician—quite the opposite—but because he understood intuitively that breakthrough politics and sustainable politics require different strategies, different skills, and different approaches to coalition-building.

After examining sixteen of the most significant primary breakthroughs since 1960, several patterns emerge that help explain why some shooting stars burn out quickly while others sustain their energy long enough to reach the White House. The first and most important insight is that in the modern primary system, breakthrough moments are not just opportunities—they are necessities. No candidate can win a presidential nomination through steady, incremental progress alone. At some point, every successful presidential campaign must create or capitalize on a moment that transforms the political dynamics of the race.

John Kennedy understood this when he gambled everything on Wisconsin and West Virginia in 1960, using victories in hostile territory to prove his electability beyond the Catholic vote. Jimmy Carter grasped it when he invested two years of his life in Iowa, converting obscurity from a liability into an asset that allowed him to introduce himself to voters on his own terms. Barack Obama recognized it when he built his entire strategy around an Iowa victory that would establish him as a credible alternative to Hillary Clinton's seemingly inevitable nomination.

Even candidates who ultimately failed to secure nominations often succeeded in creating breakthrough moments that advanced their political careers or influenced their parties' directions. Eugene McCarthy's near-victory in New Hampshire didn't lead to the presidency, but it ended Lyndon Johnson's political career and altered the course of American foreign policy. Gary Hart's "new ideas" campaign didn't win the 1984 Democratic nomination, but it established themes and constituencies that would shape Democratic politics for decades.

The breakthrough imperative reflects the fundamental economics of modern presidential campaigns. With dozens of candidates competing for limited media attention, fundraising dollars, and volunteer energy, only those who can create compelling narratives of momentum and excitement can survive the Darwinian process of primary politics. Voters, donors, and activists naturally gravitate toward candidates who seem to be winning, creating self-reinforcing cycles that reward breakthrough moments and punish steady decline.

Yet as this book has demonstrated repeatedly, creating breakthrough moments is only half the challenge facing presidential candidates. The more difficult task is converting initial success into the kind of sustained political operation that can win nominations and presidencies. This sustainability challenge explains why political history is littered with the wreckage of campaigns that briefly captured the public imagination but couldn't translate excitement into lasting political power.

The sustainability challenge manifests itself in several ways. First, breakthrough campaigns often depend on assets—charismatic personalities, compelling messages, passionate volunteers—that are difficult to scale up to national operations. Howard Dean's internet-driven grassroots energy was perfect for creating excitement and raising money, but it proved inadequate for the complex organizational challenges of competing in multiple states simultaneously. Rick Santorum's authentic conservative message and retail political skills were ideally suited for Iowa's caucus system, but they didn't translate effectively to the large, diverse primary states that ultimately determined the Republican nomination.

Second, breakthrough candidates often discover that the qualities that enabled their initial success become liabilities as campaigns progress and scrutiny intensifies. John McCain's authentic, unscripted approach to campaigning was refreshing during the breakthrough phase of his 2000 campaign, but his unwillingness to moderate his positions or temper his rhetoric limited his ability to build the broader coalitions necessary for sustained success. Pat Buchanan's provocative rhetoric generated the media attention his insurgent campaign required, but it also reinforced perceptions that he was too extreme for general election voters.

Third, breakthrough moments typically attract the kind of organized opposition from party establishments that can quickly overwhelm insurgent campaigns that lack institutional support. Gary Hart's 1984 campaign faced the full force of Walter Mondale's endorsement advantages and organizational strength once he emerged as a serious threat. Jesse Jackson's 1988 breakthrough generated establishment counterattacks that limited his ability to expand beyond his passionate but narrow base of support.

The candidates who successfully navigated from breakthrough to sustained success—Kennedy, Carter, Clinton, Obama, and Trump—shared certain characteristics that distinguished them from their less successful counterparts. First, they all possessed or developed the organizational capabilities necessary to compete effectively across multiple states with different political cultures and demographic compositions. Carter's methodical approach to primary politics, Obama's sophisticated understanding of delegate mathematics, and Trump's ability to generate free media coverage all provided sustainable advantages that could be maintained over many months of campaigning.

Second, successful breakthrough candidates managed to expand their initial coalitions without alienating their core supporters. Carter broadened his appeal from born-again Christians to include secular Democrats without losing his evangelical base. Obama attracted working-class voters and African Americans while maintaining his original coalition of college-educated professionals and young people. Trump added suburban Republicans and working-class Democrats to his initial base of populist conservatives.

Third, the successful candidates demonstrated strategic flexibility that allowed them to adapt their messages and tactics to changing circumstances without compromising their core identities. Clinton's ability to acknowledge personal flaws while maintaining his policy focus, Obama's skill in adjusting his change message to different audiences, and Trump's capacity to remain authentic while expanding his appeal all reflected the kind of tactical sophistication that sustainable success requires.

Perhaps most importantly, the successful breakthrough candidates understood that winning presidential nominations required building governing coalitions, not just movement politics. They recognized that primary elections were means to an end—capturing the presidency—rather than ends in themselves. This understanding influenced every aspect of their campaigns, from their policy positions to their personnel decisions to their media strategies.

The nature of breakthrough politics has evolved significantly since 1960, shaped by changes in media technology, campaign finance laws, and the demographic composition of the American electorate. The rise of television transformed political communication, making visual appeal and media savvy more important than ever before. The internet revolutionized fundraising and organizing, enabling candidates to build national operations without traditional institutional support. Social media created new opportunities for direct voter contact while also accelerating the pace of political communication and the speed with which narratives could change.

Each technological shift created new paths to breakthrough while closing off others. Kennedy's mastery of television gave him decisive advantages over opponents who relied on radio and print media. Dean's internet innovations provided capabilities that had never existed before, though they proved insufficient for sustained success. Obama's integration of online and offline organizing represented the maturation of digital political technologies. Trump's Twitter-driven media strategy demonstrated how social media platforms could be weaponized for political advantage.

The demographic evolution of American politics has also influenced breakthrough dynamics. The civil rights movement, women's liberation, and increasing racial and ethnic diversity have created new constituencies and new opportunities for candidates who can appeal to previously marginalized communities. Jesse Jackson's Rainbow Coalition, Barack Obama's multiracial alliance, and the growing importance of suburban women in Republican primaries all reflect these demographic changes.

Yet technological and demographic changes have also created new challenges for breakthrough candidates. The proliferation of media choices has fragmented political audiences, making it more difficult to create the kind of shared breakthrough moments that dominated earlier eras. The increasing polarization of American politics has reduced the number of truly independent voters who might be attracted to insurgent candidacies. The rise of negative advertising and opposition research has made it more difficult for breakthrough candidates to maintain the kind of positive momentum that their campaigns require.

One of the most sobering lessons from this examination of breakthrough politics is the personal cost that such campaigns exact from candidates and their families. The intensity required to create and sustain breakthrough moments—the relentless travel, the constant scrutiny, the emotional highs and lows—places enormous stress on individuals who are often unprepared for the psychological demands of modern presidential politics.

Several breakthrough candidates in this book struggled with the personal dimensions of their political success. Gary Hart's personal life became a subject of national scrutiny that ultimately destroyed his political career. Howard Dean's emotional investment in his campaign contributed to the breakdown that culminated in the infamous "Dean Scream." John McCain's legendary temper, while sometimes an asset in creating authentic moments, also became a liability when it suggested he lacked the emotional control necessary for presidential leadership.

The families of breakthrough candidates also pay significant prices for their spouses' or parents' political ambitions. The Santorum family's decision to bring their dying son, Gabriel, home from the hospital became a powerful testament to their pro-life convictions, but it also subjected them to a level of personal scrutiny that few families could endure. The Obama family's adjustment to life in the public eye required sacrifices that were largely invisible to the voters who benefited from Barack Obama's political success.

Even successful breakthrough candidates often express ambivalence about the costs of their political success. Bill Clinton's remarkable resilience in overcoming scandal after scandal came at the price of a complicated relationship with truth-telling that would haunt his presidency. Donald Trump's ability to generate controversy and media attention transformed American politics, but it also contributed to a level of political polarization that has damaged democratic institutions and social cohesion.

Despite these costs, breakthrough politics serves essential functions in American democracy that justify its continued importance in presidential selection. First, breakthrough campaigns provide mechanisms for political renewal that allow the system to adapt to changing circumstances and emerging challenges. Without Eugene McCarthy's anti-war insurgency, the Democratic Party might never have confronted the failures of its Vietnam policy. Without Pat Buchanan's populist challenge, the Republican Party might not have recognized the growing alienation of its working-class supporters.

Second, breakthrough politics creates opportunities for talented individuals who might otherwise be excluded from consideration for the presidency due to their lack of traditional credentials or institutional support. Barack Obama's 2008 campaign demonstrated that exceptional political talent could overcome disadvantages in experience and establishment connections. Pete Buttigieg's 2020 breakthrough showed that even small-city mayors could compete seriously for the presidency if they possessed the right combination of skills and strategic insight.

Third, breakthrough campaigns often articulate ideas and represent constituencies that might otherwise be marginalized in political discourse dominated by established leaders and conventional wisdom. Jesse Jackson's emphasis on economic justice and racial equality, Howard Dean's early opposition to the Iraq War, and Nikki Haley's vision of conservative politics beyond Trump all contributed to political conversations that might not have occurred without their insurgent candidacies.

The breakthrough imperative also serves as a check on political establishments that might otherwise become complacent or disconnected from the concerns of ordinary voters. The constant possibility that insurgent candidates might emerge to challenge established leaders forces parties and politicians to remain responsive to changing public opinion and evolving political circumstances.

As American politics continues to evolve, the dynamics of breakthrough campaigns will undoubtedly change as well, shaped by new technologies, demographic shifts, and institutional developments that are difficult to predict. However, several trends seem likely to influence the future of presidential primary politics.

The continued fragmentation of media audiences will probably make it more difficult to create the kind of shared breakthrough moments that characterized earlier eras of American politics. Future candidates may need to master multiple communication platforms simultaneously, appealing to different audiences through different channels while maintaining consistent core messages. The rise of artificial intelligence and automated content creation may create new opportunities for sophisticated campaigns while also making it more difficult for authentic voices to break through algorithmic noise.

The increasing diversity of the American electorate will create new opportunities for breakthrough candidates who can appeal to emerging demographic groups while also requiring more complex coalition-building strategies than previous generations of politicians needed to master. Future breakthrough campaigns will need to navigate not just racial and ethnic diversity, but also generational differences, educational polarization, and geographic fragmentation that have become increasingly important in American politics.

The continued evolution of campaign finance laws and technologies will influence which candidates can compete effectively for presidential nominations. The rise of small-dollar fundraising has democratized political finance in ways that benefit insurgent candidates, but the increasing importance of super PACs and outside spending has also created new advantages for candidates with wealthy supporters or institutional backing.

Perhaps most importantly, the health of American democratic institutions will influence whether breakthrough politics continues to serve constructive functions or becomes a destructive force that undermines political stability. The Trump presidency demonstrated how breakthrough politics could challenge institutional norms in ways that strengthened democratic participation while also threatening democratic governance. Future breakthrough candidates will need to navigate the tension between disrupting failed establishments and preserving the institutional foundations that make democratic politics possible.

Ultimately, the story of presidential primary breakthroughs is the story of American democracy itself—its capacity for renewal, its openness to change, and its ability to elevate unlikely leaders when circumstances demand new approaches to persistent challenges. The shooting stars examined in this book represent both the promise and the peril of democratic politics, demonstrating how quickly political fortunes can change while also revealing the constraints that limit even the most talented politicians.

The breakthrough candidates who succeeded in reaching the presidency—Kennedy, Carter, Clinton, Obama, and Trump—proved that American politics remains open to dramatic change when the right candidates appear at the right moments with the right strategies. Their success validates the democratic faith that political power ultimately belongs to the people, who retain the ability to overturn any establishment that fails to serve their needs or represent their values.

The breakthrough candidates who fell short of their ultimate goals—from Eugene McCarthy to Nikki Haley—nonetheless contributed to the ongoing evolution of American political thought and practice. Their campaigns expanded the boundaries of political possibility, introduced new ideas and constituencies into national discourse, and demonstrated that the American political system remains capable of producing surprises that confound conventional wisdom and challenge entrenched power.

The tension between breakthrough and sustainability that defines this book reflects broader tensions within democratic politics between innovation and stability, between popular participation and institutional competence, between the demands of campaigning and the requirements of governing. These tensions cannot be resolved definitively because they are inherent in the democratic process itself. They can only be managed through the kind of political leadership that understands both the necessity of change and the importance of continuity.

As this book is being completed, a new generation of potential breakthrough candidates is already preparing for future presidential campaigns, studying the successes and failures of their predecessors while developing their own strategies for capturing lightning in a bottle. Some will succeed in creating breakthrough moments that briefly illuminate the political landscape before fading into obscurity. Others will discover the secret of converting initial success into sustained political power that can be used to govern effectively and address the challenges facing American society.

The cycle will continue because it must continue. American democracy depends on the possibility of political renewal, the promise that new leaders can emerge to address new challenges, and the faith that breakthrough moments will continue to occur when they are most needed. The shooting stars of presidential politics serve as reminders that in a democracy, no position is permanent, no establishment is unassailable, and no dream is impossible for those who understand how to harness the forces of change, hope, and popular will that always exist beneath the surface of political life.

The next breakthrough candidates are already among us, preparing for their moments in the spotlight, studying the lessons of their predecessors, and developing the strategies that will either carry them to political success or consign them to the ranks of those who burned brightly but briefly in the constellation of American presidential politics. Their stories will add new chapters to the ongoing narrative of breakthrough and sustainability, success and failure, shooting stars and lasting suns that define the American experiment in democratic self-government.

The only certainty is that breakthrough moments will continue to occur, because they are essential to the health and vitality of democratic politics. In a system based on popular sovereignty and competitive elections, there must always be room for new voices, new ideas, and new leaders who can capture the public imagination and translate that excitement into political power. The shooting stars of presidential politics serve as proof that American democracy remains alive, dynamic, and capable of producing the leaders that each generation requires to meet its unique challenges and fulfill its distinctive promises.

The story of breakthrough politics is far from over. It is, in fact, eternal—as enduring as democracy itself and as renewable as the American capacity for political innovation and institutional adaptation. The next breakthrough is already forming somewhere in the American political landscape, waiting for the right candidate, the right moment, and the right combination of circumstances to illuminate new possibilities for American governance and democratic leadership.

The shooting stars will continue to rise, blaze across the political firmament, and either burn out quickly or sustain their light long enough to guide the nation toward new destinations. That is their purpose, their promise, and their permanent contribution to the ongoing American experiment in democratic self-government.

www.ingramcontent.com/pod-product-compliance
Lightning Source LLC
Chambersburg PA
CBHW031430270326
41930CB00007B/643

* 9 7 8 1 9 6 9 8 2 6 0 5 4 *